Contents

11th September 2001

I wish to dedicate this book to the boys and girls, men and women who lost their lives in the terrorist attacks in New York, Washington and Pittsburgh on the 11th September 2001. Many of those totally innocent people worked in the financial services industry and made the ultimate sacrifice whilst simply doing their job.

It matters not whether they were colleagues who we knew: they were our brothers and sisters in a truly global industry. Their loss and the suffering of their loved ones will be felt by everyone of us, no matter what part of the industry we work in, for a very long time.

David Loader, September 2001

Preamble

In this book I hope to be able to take the reader through some of the many, many issues and some of the detail that will be important in a manager or supervisor role. There will be areas of the book that will not cover subjects in great detail and areas of a vast industry that are hardly mentioned. Therefore there are work sessions that I suggest which will enhance the learning process as you carry out your research.

The role and responsibilities of supervising and managing an operations team in global markets should not be underestimated and if you are seeking to take the Securities Institute examinations you will need to work hard on the additional research suggested.

That said it is, believe me, well worth while as the challenges you will face will be *real* challenges and the satisfaction of successfully establishing your management style and delivering the objectives set for you will be great.

Remember always that you never stop learning, lead by example, listen to others and accept that you are not always right!

I wish you well for the future.

Thanks to: *the DSC.portfolio* and *Derivative Management Services Ltd*

ABOUT THE AUTHOR

David Loader is actively involved in the international financial markets as a Director of The Derivatives and Securities Consultancy Ltd, Computer Based Learning Ltd and Derivatives Management Services Ltd. With over twenty five years experience in the financial services industry, much of the time at senior management level including operations director within major investment banks including Warburg Securities, SBC Warburg and Warburg Futures and Options Ltd.

David is heavily involved with all three companies of which he is a director providing a variety of services in training and consultancy to a broad base of clients worldwide. He designs and delivers training courses at all levels on many areas of the financial markets and in particular those related to operations. He has been commissioned to deliver programs to audiences in a variety of countries for industry organisations such as the Singapore Exchanges, The Stock Exchange of Thailand, the Australian Financial Markets Association and the Malaysian Exchanges. In addition to his work for clients in the United Kingdom, he has delivered training and consultancy in centres such as Milan, Prague, Singapore, Hong Kong, Boston, New York, Bermuda, Mumbai, Sydney, Johannesburg, Brussels and Frankfurt.

David is Managing Director of The Derivatives and Securities Consultancy Ltd, an affiliate member of the Securities Institute. (SIAff) a member of the Institute of Directors (IOD) and also a member of The Guild of International Bankers. Since 1999, David has been involved in CBL, which has been developed as a sister company to DMS Ltd. David is the senior author of CBL's visUlearn products, which cover the financial services industry. His practical knowledge of the financial industry is combined with his unique teaching ability culminating in the innovative visUlearn range of multimedia training products.

FUNDAMENTALS OF
GLOBAL OPERATIONS MANAGEMENT

1

OPERATIONS MANAGEMENT

The management of operations in organisations within the financial services industry is a diverse challenge. The complexity of todays financial markets is reflected not only in the provision of the operational support and administration functions within major banks, fund management companies and brokers, but also in private investment, corporate business and the administering of the government in many countries. Trading and investment strategies become ever more innovative as new products are developed to hedge, speculate, arbitrage and invest. With each new product comes the need to administer the transaction, to clear and settle the trades so that the legal ownership is recorded and the relevant payments made. As the complexity of trading and investment increases so the demands on the operational teams that support the business grows. And yet it is wrong to assume that the sole function of an operations team is settlement.

Today there are many specialist functions within the overall operations remit. Client services, risk management, regulatory, profit generation and retention and the marketing/sales of "operations" products. The deregulation of many financial markets around the world has lead to an explosion in transactions not in domestic products but in international products and markets. This move into cross border trading is followed by cross border settlement. The latter is infinitely more complex than the trading.

Through the '70s, '80s and early 1990s, the changes in the front office environment, particularly the growth of electronic and telephone dealing, growing international investment, the competitive environment created by the de-regulation, the increase in the volumes of business and a growing need for greater regulation and protection for the private investor, all impacted significantly on the operations function. Dematerialised settlement saw less paper in the office, computer systems became central to the clearing and settlement process, international securities depositories reduced some of the problems and risk in settling cross border trades. Industry bodies created guidelines for standard messaging formats, encouraged the use of uniform agreements and advocated facilities such as dematerialised (electronic book-entry non-paper settlement), rolling settlement instead of account settlement and stock lending and borrowing to help reduce the problems of settlement failing to happen on the due date.

However, the real catalyst for the dramatic change in the operations function came with the growth in the use of products like derivatives where an administrative error or the failure to pick up on a dealing error could result in six figure losses, and worse!

Ironically, derivatives were not exactly new instruments, their origins being back in the middle-ages. What was new was the explosion in growth of financial derivatives, some relatively simple in concept like futures and options, others much more complex and bespoke.

It would be the combination of a dealer and derivative products that would ultimately bring about a complete rethink on the importance of operations, but firms were also conscious of the need for greater technology to be available in the support areas to service the burgeoning business being created in trading and investment. There were also significant changes taking place in the markets themselves and particularly in the use of technology.

The London Stock Exchange introduced the Talisman system and later CREST (after a debacle over another system Taurus). The London International Financial Futures and Options Exchange (LIFFE) moved from open-outcry to electronic dealing through the LIFFE CONNECT™ system. LIFFE clears through the London Clearing House (LCH) its derivative products in what is now completely electronic process and both the London Metal Exchange and the International Petroleum Exchange, now part of the Intercontinental Exchange (ICE), also use LCH to clear their trades. (In late 2001 LIFFE announced it had accepted an offer from Euronext, the combined derivatives exchanges and bourses of Holland, Belgium and France, and in 2002 became part of that exchange. Subsequently LCH and Euronext have discussed creating the largest pan-European clearing organisation by linking LCH with Clearnet, the Euronext clearing house.) In Germany the stock exchange and derivative exchange clearing has been merged into a single organisation, Clearstream that also encompasses one of the first international central securities depositories, Cedel. Subsequently Euroclear, another major international central securities depository, absorbed SICOVAM the French depository and through various shareholdings is closely linked into Clearnet and Euronext. This means that there are two large groupings of exchanges, clearing houses and depositories in Europe and as a result the streamlining of the clearing and settlement process is rapidly occurring. Elsewhere there are more developments such as the Nordic Alliance, Portugal's markets scheduled to be joining Euronext in 2002 and the London Stock Exchange having failed to persuade LIFFE to accept its offer is talking in earnest with the US market Nasdaq.

So much change is of course both creating short term problems for operations teams, but generating longer term a more structured and simplified clearing and settlement process. To illustrate some of the slightly confusing situations that exist and will need to be resolved, we have:

- LCH, which is talking about linking into Euronext's Clearnet, is providing a central counterparty clearing services to CREST for some London Stock Exchange transactions, however the LSE is talking about merging with Nasdaq having seemingly rejected linking to Euronext.
- LIFFE which has become part of Euronext is also linked to Nasdaq to trade share futures contracts via *Nasdaq LIFFE Markets* the first US exchange to list share futures

The process of rationalisation, links, alliances, take-overs (many exchanges are switching from being mutual memberships to publicly quoted companies) and mergers still has many possibilities and permutations to be played out.

Change is not confined to Europe. In the Far East the stock exchanges and derivative exchanges of both Singapore and Hong Kong have joined to create The Singapore Exchange (SGX) and Hong Kong Exchanges and Clearing (HKEx). In the US the big three derivative markets, the Chicago Board of Trade, Chicago Mercantile and

Chicago Board of Trade have participated in a joint venture whilst the New York Mercantile Exchange has offered to buy the London Metal Exchange.

There is much more going on and changes will continue to happen around the world for some years to come.

Other influences on the role and structure of operations have occurred and in particular the impact of this event that occurred in the derivatives market.

In 1995, Nick Leeson a former back office employee who became a qualified derivatives dealer in the Singapore office of Barings, changed forever the role and profile of operations.

In the aftermath of the collapse of the bank, it became clear that operations was not only a very critical means of risk control over the front office activities, but it was also a major source of risk for a business in its own right.

The need to have independent verification of the trades, positions and financial movements associated with dealing was not simply administration and bookkeeping. Fundamentally it is the key control, reconciling the actual market situation against the deal records and if it is inefficient, fails or is non-existent the whole business is put at risk.

Today this role is recognised and thus from perhaps a humble background, operations is now up there alongside the front office. In many of the more enlightened organisations there is mutual respect for the professionalism of their operations and a realisation that teamwork is not a cliché but a reality for a successful business.

So key factors that are changing the role of the operations team are the changes to the regulatory environment in the UK and elsewhere and the recognition of operational risk as we mentioned earlier. On the one hand we are looking at more professionalism and qualified personnel in operations teams and on the other a crucial role in the risk management of the business. Business skills as well as product knowledge are the requirements of managers and supervisors in today's globalised, diverse and ever expanding financial markets arena. The business skills are to manage budgets, personnel, risk management and global trading and investment. Above all, the operations manager must be able to manage time and possess coaching and motivational skills.

Product knowledge is to ensure that the increasingly integrated use of instruments, the development of systems and critical projects such as straight through processing can be managed successfully in the hurly burly of the daily routines.

To a business in the financial markets an inefficient operations function is pure risk. A top operations manager is worth, and today is paid, a significant amount. So they should be given the diversity of the role. Part business developer, part risk manager, part people manager and relationship manager to internal and external parties, the operations managers time is unlikely to fall into the leisurely category. Even in "quiet" market conditions the operational functions continue uninterrupted.

Operations is still about routine and administration and record keeping, but today it is much more than this. For the operations manager it is a huge and demanding challenge and one that keeps growing as the global financial markets come within the reach of all.

WORK SESSION

Significant changes have taken place in the industry and are still happening now. What are two significant ones that will or have impacted on your organisation?

2

MARKETS

Securities markets exist in all the mature and most of the emerging countries. As such they offer investors, speculators and traders many opportunities but also a challenge in the settlement and administration of transactions.

The characteristics of different securities products create different clearing, settlement and safekeeping requirements. In recent years, efforts to standardise the clearing and settlement processes have seen some success. The Group of 30 (G30), a private sector industry group set up in 1978 to look at the workings of the financial markets and to examine the international repercussions of decisions taken which affect the financial sector. It is a non-profit international body with senior representatives of the private and public sectors as well as academics. G30 puts on seminars and symposia and produces papers to debate certain issues. It published recommendations back in the late 1980s covering Securities Settlement and Clearance and Derivatives Practices and Principles. G30 is funded by contributions from foundations, banks, corporations, central banks and individuals. The International Securities Services Association (ISSA), is another forum which was set up in 1979 for operations professionals to exchange information and ideas with regard to the international securities markets. The members, who represent a major share of cross-border investment business, meet regularly to share information, co-operate and importantly to explore new ideas and models for improvements in the securities services sector. ISSA carried out a review of the level of compliance with the G30 recommendations and in 2000, ISSA published a new set of recommendations. Both the original G30 recommendations and the ISSA 2000 recommendations seek to improve the efficiency of the settlement process and to therefore reduce operational risk.

Despite the advances in creating a more uniform settlement process for securities, there are still numerous different practices in place. One key issue is the settlement convention, the date on which transactions would normally be expected to settle in a particular market. Commonly shown as T (trade day) + X (number of days) the convention for equities, bonds, derivatives and money market transactions varies considerably across product and country.

In February 2001 the UK moved from T+5 to T+3 for equity settlement. However government bond transactions in the UK settle T+1 and corporate bonds T+3, exchange traded derivatives settle T+1 whilst spot foreign exchange deals settle 2 business days later

There are historical precedents for the settlement convention applicable to certain types of product.

Bearer securities (mainly bonds) can effectively settle immediately as title or ownership passes on the handing over of the security whilst registered securities (mainly equities) take longer as the change of ownership needs to be made by a third party, the Registrar who maintains the record of the ownership of issued shares on behalf of the company. In traditional certificated settlement environments this entails the completion of a document the transfer form and the forwarding of it with the physical certificate to the registrar. This obviously takes time but today the impact of electronic markets, dematerialised (paperless) settlement and the use of electronic instructions between clearing house and registrar means that even with registered securities ownership, details can be updated within a very short time. Exchange traded derivatives are registered in the sense that there is a record maintained of the holders of the derivative positions but in this case it is the member firm of the clearing house who may not be the "actual" owner ie, a fund management client of the member broker.

When one considers that the sophistication of users of the financial markets means that frequently a trading strategy or investment decision may involve more than one type of security, the lack of commonality in both characteristic and settlement convention inevitably leads to operational issues.

Consider the following example:

Fund manager of an international fund with a base currency in US$ adopts the following strategy. Having decided that there is a profit on the BT shares that will generate cash for other investment strategies, but not wishing to lose the exposure to BT shares the fund manager:

1. Sells 200,000 British Telecom shares that will settle T+3
2. Buys 200 (representing 200,000 shares) BT Call options that will settle T+1
3. Sells £ and Buys US$ spot for settlement in 2 days.

Sterling cash for the settlement of the Sterling/dollar foreign exchange (FX) deal and purchase of the option will come from the sale of the shares but that will be a day after the FX deal is due to settle and two days after the option is due to settle.

It is a funding issue for both the client and the broker.

The client, because they have a mismatch on the cash flow and will need either other cash or a borrowing facility. The broker because as the party recognised by the clearing house they are liable to the clearing house for the settlement of the option whether or not the client has the cash available.

This situation would be further complicated if, for some reason, the sale of the shares fails to take place on the settlement date, T+3. Any delay would add to the costs of the strategy unless the circumstances enable some kind of claim to be made against a third party causing the delay.

In chapter 1 the importance of product knowledge was mentioned. Given the diversity of the instruments available in the financial and commodity markets there is a significant problem for the operations manager. It is important for the manager to have not only a wide knowledge of the key elements of the main markets but to also be able to staff the operation with adequate specialist knowledge. The key question is how much knowledge should the manager have?

It depends on the nature of the business and the structure within the organisation. In a large international bank the structure may be along product lines whereas in a fund management company there may be less segregation of product line within the operations area at least. This leads to, in the first case, specialists in equity, fixed income, derivatives etc., the latter may also be split between on and off-exchange. Whereas in the fund management company the need for broad based product knowledge at manager level is crucial.

Developing your personal knowledge level and at the same time developing the right knowledge level in the team is one of the more challenging tasks the operations manager faces.

We look at the detailed aspects of clearing and settlement in chapter 5 but let us look at the major securities markets and in doing so we can start with the market most people are at least familiar with, the equity market.

Equity Securities

Equity markets have seen significant activity in the past decade as interest rates have stabilised in the major economies and the return on equities has grown. The huge activity has not been without problems, with many organisations experiencing problems in keeping their operational functions adequately resourced to deal with the growth in volumes. With the growth in equities being experienced not only in the mature markets, but also in the emerging markets, there has been significant pressure put on the managers and teams in operations

Part of the return on an equity security is of course the dividend with the capital gain being generated by the increase in the share price. The buoyant market has led to many new issues, rights issues, mergers and takeovers as companies seek to exploit the investors desire for a home for their money. In some cases the intense activity has created liquidity problems.

Liquidity in a security is an important aspect of the market. The ability to trade, ie, there being enough participants to meet buying and vice-versa selling demand is important, but so is the ability to settle those transactions. As organisations and individuals trade the security every transaction creates a settlement process.

With high and potentially frequent turnover amongst the participants, there is a danger that the settlement processes will not keep pace and therefore settlement on the due date does not take place. Quickly a knock on effect happens as delayed settlements in turn create delays for other settlements and so on. Liquidity in trading terms can, and often does, create liquidity problems in settlement terms. The successful management of this process is an important one for the operations managers and supervisors. We look at various ways in which liquidity issues can be resolved later in the book but we need to mark this point down as an operational risk.

Equity securities are a source of numerous processes from issuance to distribution of benefits like dividends. Much can happen with a share and many of these events may require a decision to be made either in the front or back office (or both) or by a third party like a client.

The company that issues the shares is sometimes the driver of the processes. For instance, the actual terms of the shares can dictate the subsequent events that impact in the operations area.

Consider the following types of share:

- Ordinary Share or Common Stock
- Preference Share
- Deferred Share
- Designated shares ie, "A" or "B" shares
- Non-voting and Restricted Shares.

A company that issues ordinary shares is seeking to raise capital in return for a stake in the company's fortunes. The potential investor will need to decide whether this company represents a reasonable investment. The prospectus that the company issues is therefore of paramount importance as it provides the information on which the investors judgement is made.

The reason that capital markets exist is to raise capital and provide investment opportunity. Not all investors possess the same requirements in terms of a return on their money. Hence we have people who are considered "conservative" in their approach and others who are more "speculative". Obviously there has to be a variety of investment products for these differing views and expectations.

But just as important are the views of an organisation seeking to raise capital. To issue equity shares raises money but gives away some ownership and control. That may not be desirable or necessary as far as the board of the organisation is concerned.

So, in the capital markets we have two drivers behind the kind of products available, the issuers of securities and the investors.

From the company point of view, the issue must be attractive to both the company itself and to the potential investor. An investor may be happy to have a stake in a company but does not want the uncertainty of dividend flows. The company can overcome this by issuing not just ordinary shares but preferred shares giving more certainty to the investor but at the cost of a (often) fixed liability.

The terms of the issue are therefore extremely important not only to the company and the investor, but also to those involved in the settlement process. A dividend may be paid on an ordinary share, it is more likely to be paid on a preference share, and may be related to a previous period as preference shareholders have the right to their dividend ahead of the ordinary shareholders.

Deferred Shares are different again, the terms conferring different rights and timings to voting and dividend income.

"A" and "B" shares will have different voting rights and sometimes different dividend payments.

At the time of issue the company offers the product and the investor makes the choice. Thereafter it is down to the operations teams in different organisations and the investor themselves to understand what processes and actions are needed for the product traded.

It becomes clear that information is critically important to the whole trading, investment, settlement, clearing and safe custody process associated with the securities markets and the capital markets

We need to define the "capital markets" to understand where securities fit in and to illustrate the complexity of products, investment, participation and support roles.

Capital Markets

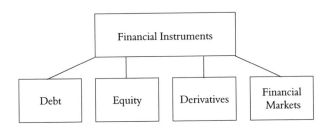

Figure 2.1

Investment Cycle

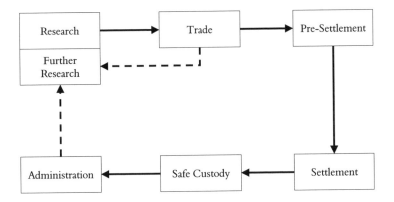

Figure 2.2

The Industry Relationships

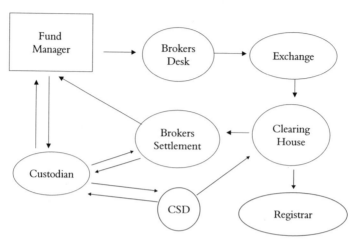

Figure 2.3

From the preceding diagrams we begin to see just how varied the products and participants are. In fig 2.3 for instance we see how the fund manager places an order to the brokers desk. From there the order is completed on the exchange is cleared by the clearing house and then, for a registered security, the ownership change is recorded by the registrar and or the central securities depository (CSD) and the brokers settlement team liaise with the fund manager for the relevant settlement amounts. Some of the settlement process and the custody/safekeeping services will often be managed by a custodian or CSD on behalf of the fund manager. We have already seen how a strategy might involve the equity, derivative and foreign exchange markets. Markets exist to service the requirements of users like corporate entities, investors, traders and hedgers and the many kinds of strategies they utilise.

Markets are either "real" in the sense that there is a formal structure and location or are colloquially referred to as markets. The foreign exchange market is an example of the latter, the "market" being counterpart to counterpart or over-the-counter, whereas the London Stock Exchange is an example of the former, securities trades being dealt within the rules, regulations and facilities of the exchange. It is also important to remember that products traded on an exchange (on-exchange) can also sometimes be traded off-exchange.

Markets also exist where there is a place designated for people to trade face to face, whilst other markets are electronic.

An example of a new market, which is useful to examine, is JIWAY. It is an integrated electronic European stock exchange which is focused on the needs of retail investors, although they are not involved directly, they have to use brokers, financial advisors and other intermediaries to access the market. JIWAY offers real time trading and settlement on major US and European equities. It is owned by the OM Group, Sweden.

From the operations managers' point of view, the source of the trade is as important as the product itself, not least because the settlement convention may differ as a result of being traded on or off exchange.

Securities markets are commonly those that are associated with equities and bonds. We have talked about equities and before moving on to consider the characteristics of bonds we need to understand some key features of equities.

UK EQUITIES: KEY FEATURES

Security:	Share of Ownership
Issued By:	Private and Public Companies
Method of Issue:	Authorised Share Capital
Type of Issue:	Private offering, Public Offering, Placement
Issue Document:	Prospectus
Traded:	On and Off Exchange
Type:	Usually Registered Shares (can be Bearer)
Income:	Dividend
Unit of Trading:	One Share (can be different ie, 50 shares)
Duration:	In existence for the life of the corporation ie, until the shares are bought back by the company or the company ceases to exist (bankruptcy, take-over, merger, nationalisation)

In the Memorandum and Articles of Association of a company is the Authorised share capital. This authorised share capital will be made up of designated shares, for example "ordinary 25p shares". The 25p is the nominal value of the shares and they cannot be issued for less than that, although of course they can and often are issued at a higher price.

Shares can be issued privately as is the case with a small company (a company must have at least two shareholders) in which case they are usually "Limited" (Ltd), a term that refers to the liability that the company has (but not the liability of the Directors). If the shares are offered for sale to the general public via a listing on a stock exchange they are usually "Public Limited Companies" (PLC).

A Prospectus is issued that contains relevant information that enables the potential shareholder to make an assessment of the merits of subscribing for the shares at the price the company is wishing to provide them at (the "offer price").

The prospectus must be factual, not make misleading or unrealistic projections and must detail the business profile, directors profiles, any past trading history, projections for the future and the number of shares already in issue and being offered.

The Prospectus will state whether the shares are being offered "fully paid" or "partly paid", the former meaning the full value of the shares at the offer price must be paid on application, the latter meaning that a portion of the value is paid on application and the remainder in one or more stages.

Details of the method of applying for shares, the timetable, issuing agents etc must also be included.

An example of a partly paid issue would be British Telecom plc that was privatised by the UK government and in order to encourage private individuals to invest the offer price was split into three separate "calls". As a further incentive to the private investor and to encourage long-term investment, Bonus shares (shares issued free of charge) were offered to those investors who purchased shares under the original offer and held them for a period of time.

Any "New Issue" of shares requires an operations team to be aware of the details and particularly the critical times such as the closing date for applications, amount of payment etc.

In some cases there is no offer price and instead a tender is made. Tenders are more common in bond issues and require the investor to state how much they will pay for the shares. The highest offers are then successful.

The offer to sell shares is not always matched by the investor take up and so we have over-subscribed issues, where applications for too many shares are received and under-subscribed issues where the opposite has occurred. In the case of the former, details of how such an over-subscription would be dealt with will be included in the prospectus.

Typically this will result in a scaling of allocation of shares based on a formula agreed by the company and its issuing agent. This scaling may favour institutions or small shareholders.

To protect against an under-subscription the company may have the issue under written. Here the agent or more likely a syndicate agree to take up any shares not applied for by the public. There will be a fee for this as clearly the underwriters are taking a risk. Market timing and correct pricing of an issue is crucial and many issues have failed or indeed been cancelled as a result of a sudden change in the market sentiment.

The shares we have been talking about here are being offered in the "Primary" market. To be offered on the stock exchange the offering must meet the criteria of the particular exchange. A full listing on the main market will have many conditions. Growing and new companies in the UK are able to apply for listing in other markets such as the Alternative Investment Market (AIM). The market is under the auspices of the Stock Exchange but the criteria for a listing is less onerous. Thus a company listed on AIM might be more attractive to a speculative investor who is prepared to take some risk in return for potential growth in the company.

TechMark on the LSE lists innovative technology companies, as these companies have unique requirements. It is a market within a market made up of companies of any size which share a common commitment to technological innovation. In Frankfurt we have the Neuer Markt separate from the main Bourse which lists high growth and technology companies.

Once listed in the Primary market the shares will now trade in the "Secondary" market. These are not new shares but simply the shares in existence. Trading takes place on either an "order" driven market or a "quote" driven market. Order driven markets transact business if and when a matching buy and sell order is in the market. Quote markets have a system whereby market participants, often called market makers, make bid and offer prices at which they will buy and sell shares.

When a company has issued shares into a market, any subsequent further issue of shares to raise money is offered to the existing shareholders first. This right, hence the term "Rights Issue" does not have to be taken up, it will depend on the shareholders views and means. Rights not taken up can be sold in the market by the shareholder entitled to them or by the company, the shareholder receiving the monetary value.

Rights are offered on a basis, for example 2 new shares of every 5 currently held. The rights will be at a discount to the current share price. If a company is seeking new capital in a weak situation, ie, poor performance the discount will be greater than a company making a rights issue from a position of strength.

Other types of actions, rights and other actions are known as Corporate Actions, can occur with equities. A company can issue shares free of charge so that the number of issued shares is increased and the price of the company's shares in the market will subsequently be reduced. This is sometimes called a Bonus Issue.

A company can have a share split whereby it has one million £1 shares and changes them to two million 50p shares, it could be involved in a merger or take-over whereby there will be either an agreement or the take-over will be called "hostile" or unwanted.

If a company has surplus cash it might offer to buy back some or all of its shares.

We can see how intricate the business of trading and investing in equities can be. We also need to remember that the processes and conventions in the UK are not necessarily those of other equity markets around the world.

The size of the equity markets can be seen from the following table:

Value of Business on Equity Markets 2001			
Market	**Location**	**Main Products & Indices**	**Value of Business 2001**
NASDAQ/AMEX	United States	4,100 household name companies and aspiring household names. NASDAQ Composite Index	$749.049 billion
New York Stock Exchange	United States	A cross-section of leading U.S. companies, midsize and small capitalization companies. Also non-U.S. issuers. Dow Jones	$10.5 trillion
London Stock Exchange	United Kingdom	UK and International companies covering over 60 countries. FTSE 100	£1,909,699.3 million
Tokyo Stock Exchange	Japan	2118 domestic companies and 36 International companies. Also equity and bond futures and options. TOPIX	¥217,026 billion
Deutsche Borse	Germany	Domestic companies traded in segments. International companies traded on Xetra Stars. Derivatives traded on Eurex. DAX 30	€4,408,752.47 million
Euronext	France, Belgium & Netherlands	1,539 European companies listed. Also bonds, derivatives and commodities. Euronext 100 NEXT 150	€1,668 billion
Hong Kong Exchanges	China	Equities, bonds, unit trusts, exchange traded funds and warrants. Hang Seng Index	HK$1,950 billion

Table 2.1

The business carried out on the major global equity markets is not purely domestic. Today investors, fund managers and traders transact business on a global basis, seeking to achieve growth and to maximise opportunities in the global economies.

With electronic markets and technology aiding dealers, there is no longer any boundaries to trading and investing in equities, save perhaps the regulatory and risk issues and of course certain operational constraints that global trading and investing might create such as time-zones, different settlement conventions etc. We can see this by the diversity of funds and investment trusts that invest in global markets.

The investor correspondingly can diversify risk by selecting a particular global fund or by having a portfolio of funds based on different regional markets, ie, North America, European and Asia Pacific. This has to be tempered by the fact that the globalisation of equity trading and investment is allied with a globalisation of business. A simple look at the extent of international ownership of businesses in the UK illustrates this.

However the important point is that the global economy is just that, and significantly the global economy is still driven by the US economy. Therefore any problem with the US economy is likely to impact on other economies around the world. That said, as we saw following the market crash of 1987, the performance of different equity markets varies. Today of course we also have a far greater use of derivatives and so the selling pressures in a falling market are not necessarily so marked.

Emerging markets offer huge potential for speculators and investors alike and yet they do of course carry potentially a far greater risk. The ability of local emerging equity markets to withstand negative pressure be it domestically or internationally driven is significantly lower than in a mature market. There is the possibility of political pressure on the markets that may be much greater than in a mature market and as we saw in Malaysia, there can be direct government intervention in the markets by the changing of laws.

It is worth looking at the example of Malaysia. Essentially, the situation was that Malaysia was concerned that the currency speculators would turn their attention to the Ringett and would force the authorities to use interest rates and other means to try to hold the level of the currency. The impact of volatility in the currency and the "standard" methods of trying to deal with it were viewed as likely to have a more far reaching and serious consequence on the economy than the country could stand. The government decided that they would prevent this scenario by introducing an embargo on the currency (despite the International Monetary Funds [IMF] misgivings) including preventing the removal of realised gains from the country. Thus if an investor like a UK fund had a profit on a Malaysian portfolio and sold shares in the market to realise the profit and then decided to convert the Ringetts to Sterling, it would be difficult - if not impossible - to bring that profit back to the UK by selling Ringetts for Sterling.

The impact of this solution was to negate the currency speculators but to create problems for the international investment community who became reluctant to invest in the securities markets.

Equity markets are measured of course by the movement in indices. Almost every equity market has an index or indices based on shares listed on the market and some indices are not based on a single market but have constituents based in many different markets.

Three very well known indices are the FTSE 100 index in the UK, the Dow Jones in the US and the Nikkei in Japan. As benchmarks they can be viewed with some caution as they may be unrepresentative of the equity market in general. For instance the Dow Jones indices is made up of 30 shares on leading US companies, the FTSE on the other hand is the top 100 UK companies by capitalisation (the value of the issued shares at the current share price). Furthermore the constituents of the FTSE index change on a regular basis as the "bottom" companies are replaced by companies promoted from outside the top 100.

Over time this, and various mergers and restructures of constituent companies, has changed the FTSE 100 from a broad based index to one dominated by financials, and until recently, technology companies. It could be said that an investor buying a FTSE 100 index tracker fund is not therefore investing in the fortunes of companies involved in a range of activities but rather fairly specialist sectors.

In the US the Standard & Poors 500 offers a broader based index, and therefore benchmark, to the US equity market than the Dow and perhaps not surprisingly the main equity derivatives in the US are based on the S&P.

In Europe we have seen the introduction of the so called *pan-European indices*. These indices, such as the FTSE Eurotop, Morgan Stanley Capital International (MSCI) and the Dow STOXX families, represent leading equities from across Europe. For fund managers with European portfolios and/or funds this benchmark and the related derivatives allow better management of the portfolio.

Equity derivatives are important, as the growth in volumes of index and single stock futures and options illustrates. With greater investment in equities so the need to be able to both hedge and to gain leverage or gearing on investment increases. As derivatives provide the means to both hedge and increase exposure the growth is hardly surprising.

In terms of equities in emerging markets, derivatives again have a part to play, enabling investors and traders to take exposures to the equity markets without involvement in the actual markets. Index products that are listed on mature markets like the Singapore Exchanges are based on for example the Taiwanese index.

It matters little which international equity market we look at the same issues arise as those we looked at that relate to the UK equity market. So we have companies seeking to raise capital, issuing shares, primary and secondary markets, investing, trading, clearing and settlement etc.

However, equities are not everyone's cup of tea and for investors wanting the peace of mind that comes with a known rather than possible return, other types of security exist. A significant market exists not in purchasing a stake in a company but instead in lending money in return for an income and, usually, the ultimate return of the money lent. This is the *Debt market*.

Debt Securities

Equities are familiar. Most people have heard of a stock exchange and many work for companies whose shares are listed on exchanges. An increasing number, because of privatisations, building societies converting to banks and internet trading actually own shares. Most news bulletins tell us how the equity market has performed that day with a single line statement along the lines of *"the FTSE 100 closed up 220 points at 5623.5"*

The debt markets, however, are not so widely recognised.

There are lots of reasons why this is the case. Some might say they are a more technical market and not for the private investor, others point to lack of volatility (significant movement in price) particularly when interest rates are static.

Strange then that debt markets are not only huge, they are also likely to have an impact on each and every one of us and most likely that impact will be greater than the equity markets.

Who issues debt or to put it another way borrows money and why?

A list would include:

- Governments
- Supranationals
- Corporates
- Private Companies
- Local Authorities

The reasons for issuing debt can be a matter of choice or necessity.

A company for instance might prefer to issue debt to raise capital rather than issue shares which dilutes the ownership and control.

A government cannot issue shares on the country, there is no "United Kingdom PLC" and yet the government needs capital to pay for services it provides and costs it incurs. The government has tax as a source of income and it also often has investments and reserves, however it also will have times where it needs to raise additional capital. This borrowing requirement, in the UK it is called the *Public Sector Net Cash Requirement* (PSNCR), is funded by issuing short, long and sometimes medium term instruments, the most familiar of which is likely to be the government bond.

A *bond* is an instrument that often has a fixed duration and a fixed return of interest and trading in such instruments is not surprisingly referred to as the fixed income market. However there are many types of debt instrument and different types of bond some of which have variable rates of interest, some have no interest and a very few have no maturity date.

From an operations managers point of view the settlement convention for a government bond or debt instrument is shorter, for instance T+1, than most current equity settlement conventions. But equally a corporate bond in the UK would settle T+3 the same as an equity.

The income on a bond is the interest or alternatively where there is no interest paid the bond will be issued at a discount. The interest on a bond is often called a coupon for the simple reason that most bonds were and are bearer or unregistered securities and the only means of claiming the interest due was to tear off the bond a coupon representing the value of the interest and present it to the issuers paying agent for payment.

International investment in bonds that were bearer instruments was somewhat of a problem as clearly any loss, or indeed theft, of the bond was a major disaster necessitating either copious amounts of paperwork to obtain duplicate bonds or indeed the total loss of the asset. To some extent these problems were reduced by *Central Securities Depositories* (CSDs) where the bearer securities could be held. The problems with international instruments and the growing cross-border trading were responsible for bringing about a central depository for the bearer securities that were being dealt in internationally. Euroclear and Cedel Bank (later to become Clearstream) became *International Central Securities Depositories* (ICSDs)

Raising capital through debt offers an alternative for the investor. The terms of the indenture will provide the investor with details of the debt. This includes not only the maturity of the debt but also the interest or coupon if any, the frequency of payment of the coupon and other material information on specific characteristics of the debt.

For instance, the debt may be convertible, ie, the bond can be converted either on maturity or during the life of the issue into equity shares instead of having the loan repaid in cash.

The debt may be "callable" or "puttable", ie, the issuer can call or redeem the debt earlier than the maturity or where the investor can put a request or ask the issuer to redeem the debt early. The call or put may be at selected times, can be mandatory or offered as an option, and may refer to specific numbered instruments or on a general first come first served basis.

Debt is issued in much the same way as equity. There is a primary and secondary market, there are offers and placings although the public offering of debt instruments applies primarily to government bonds. In the UK you can purchase government bonds called "gilts", an abbreviation of gilt edged security, the assumption being the government would always honour its debt. Private investors can purchase Gilts, along with other National Savings products, at the post office

In reality most debt securities are destined for the "professionals" who mange portfolios of investments for the major life insurance companies, pensions funds, central government agencies that manage investments for the government, and the providers of retail products to the man or woman in the street.

Debt instruments are commonly referred to as being at the "long" or "short" end of the market. This relates to the time to maturity and is also relevant to the yield curve, a term used to describe a view of interest rates over a period of time.

Yield, the return on the investment, is an important factor The yield on a bond with 30 years to maturity is likely to be different to one that has only say a year to maturity. Equally the price is different. So to is the yield on a bond compared to the dividend yield on an equity or a cash deposit.

Yield and other more detailed analysis of securities is made in another book, Understanding Products and Trading that accompanies this one in the series.

UK BONDS: KEY FEATURES

Security:	Debt
Issued By:	Governments, Private and Public Companies, Local Authorities
Method of Issue:	Term of Indenture
Type of Issue:	Private offering, Public Offering, Placement
Issue Document:	Prospectus
Traded:	On and Off Exchange
Type:	Usually Bearer (can be Registered)
Income:	Interest (Coupon) can also be issued at a discount with no interest payment
Unit of Trading:	£100, £1000 etc
Duration:	In existence until the maturity date of the bond unless there are terms that permit the early redemption of the bond

We know that bonds are debt instruments, usually issued for a maturity several years ahead (the benchmark US Treasury Bond is issued with 30 years to maturity) and that fixed income bonds have a coupon payable either annually or semi-annually. Bonds where no interest is paid are called *Zero Coupon* bonds and are similar to other debt instruments. Issues with a year or as little as three months and sometimes a few days are often referred to as *money market instruments* as the short duration provides them with characteristics similar to cash.

A zero coupon bond is issued at, for example, £75 and the holder will receive £100 on maturity. The amount of discount is dependent on the projected yield in the market.

Some bonds do not pay a fixed rate of interest but instead the interest rate is determined from one period to the next, quarterly, half-yearly etc, These are called *floating rate bonds* or *notes*, commonly abbreviated to "FRNs".

International bonds are issued almost exclusively through placements by major banks or syndicates. Sometimes referred to as *Eurobonds*, they are offered by an issuer in a different country or countries often in a different currency. An example would be a US company, issuing the bond in Europe and Asia in British Pounds.

Major debt instruments include:

- Bonds or Loan Stock
- Bills
- Notes
- Certificates of Deposit
- Commercial Paper
- Bankers Acceptances
- Asset-Backed Bonds
- High Yield Bonds

We need to remind ourselves that most debt instruments have terms or durations until they mature or expire. This duration can be "short" three months or less and "long", anything up to 30 years of more. Short term debt, usually one year or less, is often referred to as a money market instrument and these include certificates of deposit and treasury bills. Bonds tend to have a longer time to maturity when they are issued.

The resultant settlement process flows are dictated by the nature of the instrument. These are looked at in more detail in chapter 5, but the characteristics of securities like bonds and equities are different from those of derivatives and so therefore are the processes.

Derivative Markets

Derivatives are instruments that provide both hedging and speculative properties. In general terms they are products that will or might create a transaction the terms of which are agreed today but will occur at some time in the future. They could be said to be synthetic versions of the assets on which they are based. Thus they can give an exposure to an asset or market without the need to participate in the actual underlying asset or market. They also allow an investor to gain that exposure at a fraction of the actual cost or value of the underlying asset.

This *gearing* or *leverage* is a particularly important characteristic and a failure to have systems, processes and controls over the actual exposure rather than the cost of the derivative is vitally important in risk management.

The names of some derivative products reflect this ability to agree something today to either definitely or possibly happen later and so we have *futures, forwards, options, swaps* etc.

Derivatives are traded both on and off exchange. *Exchange-traded derivatives* (ETD) are products created by and traded on exchanges. They are standardised products, called contracts or lots, with contract specifications and are traded by members of the relevant exchange either face to face, sometimes called open outcry, or by electronic trading systems.

The contract specification is crucial as it details the essential information on:

- Size of the contract and underlying asset on which it is based
- Maturity date
- The minimum price movement and value
- Settlement convention (cash or physical)
- Trading method and times.

The following is an example of contract specifications for the LIFFE Long Gilt futures contract

Unit of trading	£100,000 nominal value notional Gilt with 7% coupon
Delivery months	March, June, September, December, such that the nearest three delivery months are available for trading.
First notice day	Two business days prior to the first day of the delivery month
Last notice day	First business day after the Last Trading Day
Delivery day	Any business day in delivery month (at seller's choice)
Last trading day	11.00
	Two business days prior to the last business day in the delivery month
Quotation	Per £100 nominal
Minimum price movement (Tick size & value)	0.01 (£10)
LIFFE CONNECT™ Trading hours	08.00 - 18.00
Trading platforms	LIFFE CONNECT™ central order book applies price/time priority trading algorithm, Basis Trade Facility, Block Trade Facility
Minimum Block Trade Threshold	See Block Trade Facility - Contract Minimum Size Thresholds

Figure 2.4   Source: LIFFE website

It may be a surprise to some to learn that derivatives are not new products and in fact can be traced back to the Middle Ages. Originally based on commodities, the derivative industry we know today commenced with establishing of the Chicago Board of Trade in 1848. Growth in the use of derivatives increased sharply in the mid 1970s when financial products were introduced and in 2000 over 3.5 billion contracts were traded.

The markets are diverse in both products and size and today it is a truly global industry. It is also misunderstood with many people believing that derivatives pose unacceptable risk. These detractors would point to various industry events that have resulted in large financial losses and yet they ignore similar losses made in equities or bonds. Why is this the case?

Derivative problems can be spectacular and therefore make headlines. Just like all financial "disasters" , in the context of frequency of losses versus actual use, derivatives are no more dangerous than any other investment provided adequate controls over their use are in place. Despite this there will still be those who maintain their use is too "risky" and therefore ignore them thus potentially and perversely generating risk in their portfolios.

Given that derivatives transfer risks between those who wish to assume risk (speculators) and those who wish to remove risk (hedgers) it is not surprising that the growth in their use over the last twenty years has been spectacular.

The fund manager who is a purchaser of equity stock can hedge the risk of the share price falling by using options whilst the investor who believes the stock will rise in price can also use options to gain greater exposure to the stock for the available funds than would be the case if they purchased stock.

What is absolutely certain is the need for high quality operations to process and control derivatives business. Operations managers must be aware of the links between equity, bond, currency or money market activity and the activity in the associated derivatives.

Settlement conventions differ, different clearing houses may be involved, corporate actions in one product may affect the other and the derivative may go to physical delivery of the asset.

Accounting for derivatives may be different than for the underlying asset and the process for valuing derivatives held in portfolios needs on a basis that truly reflects the impact of the use of the derivative on the portfolio.

The global extent and diversity of derivative products can be illustrated in the following table of exchanges and leading products:

EXCHANGE	LEADING PRODUCTS
Chicago Board of Trade	T–Bond T–Note–Futures
Chicago Mercantile Exchange	Eurodollar Future
EUREX	Eurobund Future
EURONEXT	CAC40 Index Future
London Metal Exchange	Aluminium Future
New York Mercantile Exchange	Light Sweet Crude Oil Future
Singapore Exchanges - Derivatives	Eurodollar Future
Sydney Futures Exchange	Australian 3 Year Bond Future
Tokyo Stock Exchange	Japanese Government Bond Future

Table 2.2

Operations teams must fully understand the difference in characteristics and settlement conventions of the derivatives traded on and off exchange.

Exchange traded derivatives have settlement processes that are somewhat different from securities. Futures contracts trade on margin, a process whereby the actual value of the futures contract is not settled and instead a daily settlement of the change in the value of the contract is paid or received. Only if the futures contract goes to delivery will the value of the underlying be paid or received.

An option contract has a two stage settlement. The first stage involves the payment by the buyer to the seller of a premium to secure the right to do something. If that right is exercised then a second settlement takes place as the asset is either delivered or received by the buyer.

Over The Counter (OTC) derivatives are not traded on exchanges and do not therefore have standardised contracts. They are traded between two counterparties who determine the terms of the derivative, including how and when any settlement will take place. This ability to bespoke the derivative product is highly attractive and there is a huge market in OTC derivatives. A common product is a swap, where the buyer and seller agree to swap something at set periods or on the occurrence of some trigger event or benchmark. Different participants in the markets heavily use interest rate swaps, currency swaps, commodity swaps and equity swaps.

The appendices contain examples of both exchange traded and OTC derivatives use.

Foreign Exchange and Money Markets

Currency exchange movements run into billions per day as the transactions in financial markets, commerce and business are settled. The foreign exchange markets and the markets in financial paper are massive and, like securities and derivatives are global. The 2001 Triennial Central Bank Survey of Foreign Exchange and Derivatives Market Activity published by the Bank for International Settlements in April 2001 measures the average daily turnover in traditional foreign exchange markets as $1.2 trillion. Although this daily global turnover figure is massive, it reflects a 19% decline in activity compared to the last survey in April 1998. Undoubtedly the introduction of the Euro is the major contributing factor.

Many organisations will have operations teams dedicated to the clearing and settlement function. Often called "Treasury Operations", they will deal with instruments such as:

- *Bankers acceptances*
  Short term negotiable discount notes, drawn on and accepted by banks which are obliged to pay the face value amount at maturity.
- *Eligible bills*
  A bill acceptable to the Bank of England as lender of last resort
- *Certificates of Deposit*
  A short or medium term interest bearing money market instrument offered by banks. It is a low risk, low return investment vehicle.
- *Commercial Paper*
  An unsecured obligation issued by a bank or corporation to finance short term credit needs. They usually range in duration from 2 days to 9 months.

- *Treasury Bills*
  Money market instrument issued with a life of less than one year issued by the US and UK governments.
- *Domestic and International currencies*
  Any form of money in circulation. Domestic is the unit of money used in your home country. International currencies are used in countries other than your home country and require exchange to convert them into your domestic currency.
- *Currency Futures*
  Contracts calling for delivery of a specific amount of a foreign currency at a specified future date in return for a given amount of say US Dollars.
- *Structured Products*
  A type of investment product which is made up of two or more products, that seek to meet a specific investment objective.

As with securities the various products have different settlement profiles and conventions.

With currencies for instance we have both *spot* (2 day) and *forward* transactions as well as currency derivatives like options and swaps. Many money market trades are off exchange whilst some derivatives are on exchange and others off exchange . (see Glossary for definitions of these terms)

Retail and Other Products

In today's diverse financial markets there are many products that have been developed as hybrids of the "traditional" instruments.

To meet the specific requirements of clients and investors banks and investment companies have developed a whole range of bespoke and retail products.

For corporate clients we have:

- *Mergers and Acquisition services*
  Divisions of securities houses or merchant banks responsible for advising on take-over activity. Usually work with the corporate finance department and is often kept as a single unit.
- *Structured finance*
- *Asset backed securities*
  Debt obligations that are secured against some type of or specific asset for example property, mortgages.

In the retail sector we have:

- *Life funds*
  Insurance where the premiums are invested and will provide some level of return on maturity.
- *Insurance*
  A promise of financial compensation for a specified potential loss in the future. This promise is in exchange for a monthly or annual premium payment.
- *Pension*
  Fund set up by an individual, a corporation, labour union, governmental entity or other organisation to pay the pension benefits of retired workers. Pension funds invest billions of dollars annually in the securities markets and are therefore major market players.
- *ISAs*
  An individual savings account in the UK which allows tax efficient investment of up to £7,000 in each tax year. Investment can be made as a lump sum and/or regular monthly payments and be invested in cash, shares and life insurance or all 3 options.
- *Unit Trusts*
  A vehicle whereby money from a number of investors is pooled together and invested collectively on their behalf. Each owns a unit (or number of them), the value of which depends on the value of those items owned by the trust.
- *Open Ended Investment Companies (OEICs)*
  A corporate structure introduced in 1997. It is a form of collective investment vehicle which can expand without limit.

- *Guaranteed Fund*
  A fixed term investment which guarantees growth or a return of the original investment. It is a relatively conservative investment vehicle.
- *Hedge Fund*
  A fund used by wealthy private clients and institutions. It operates aggressive investment strategies including short selling, gearing, program trading, swaps, arbitrage and derivatives.

Essentially these products are combinations of other products. For example, we have pension funds that invest in equities, bonds, money market instruments and hedge funds that invest in securities, currencies, derivatives etc.

Yet the investment objective of a hedge fund is significantly different to that of a pension fund. As a result there is a different approach to trading the instruments as pension funds take generally longer term investment views, whilst hedge funds take much shorter views of the market.

For the operations manager, the processes, procedures and controls over retail transactions are different to fund management and are very different to principal trading activity.

Operations managers in the offices of a fund manager have to deal with the fund managers/dealers, agent brokers, banks, custodians, trustees and the regulators.

Therefore to reiterate the point already made, operations is about information and communication. The role of the manager is therefore complex and it is appropriate to summarise this role and the key issues that need to be addressed and understood.

OTHER PRODUCTS

Trading in individual shares is still a major part of the market activity, however there is today significant use of products that represent a single order but across many individual securities.

Examples would be a program trade, an index future or an Exchange Traded Fund. As with all products there are differences between these types of products that determine who will use them and why.

If we look first at a program or basket trade, the rationale for use is about cost and ease of executing an investment strategy. For the operations manager there is an issue about settling such a product. From the trading side there is a single bargain but the constituents of that bargain will settle as multiple securities. Without their own basket settlement capabilities, any cost reductions will be unlikely to be achieved.

Traded funds offer investors another way to diversify their investments and minimise the impact of market fluctuations.

Market and Product Knowledge

There are many changes and developments taking place in markets and exchanges around the world. Keeping track of these changes and applying the necessary procedures and controls are issues the manager needs to address.

The key issues in respect of markets include:

*   *The structure of the market*
    It is vital for operations managers to understand how each market is structured and the legal aspects under which the market operates. Issues within the structure of the market, include the regulation applicable, the membership and the trading and settlement processes. Managers must be fully aware of their own obligations in respect of the market if they are members directly.

*   *The processes for transactions on the market*
    This includes the method of trading on the exchange, the access to the exchange and the technology available to process transactions. Managers need to ensure that there are clear communication channels with the market and that they are fully aware of new products and developments in the markets. This is particularly in relation to how it affects their own business and clients.

- *The processes for clearing and settlement*
  The way in which transactions are cleared and settled on an exchange must be an efficient process. There need to be clear rules laid down in order to deal with trades which fail to settle in the normal course of business.

- *The role of the Clearing House*
  The relationship between the exchange and the Clearing House is very important and has to work well in order to operate an efficient market. The issues which need to be considered in relation to the Clearing House are risk management, treasury, collateral management and default policies.

- *The use of markets and products by end-user clients*
  Users of the markets are either direct or indirect participants the latter often referred to as "end-users". Over the years the sophistication of the end-user has grown significantly and with technology and outsource services like fund administration and prime brokerage available such as the extent and diversity of the end-users activity has grown. In turn this has raised and continues to do so issues about services offered, risk, multi-currency capabilities etc.

- *The role of industry associations*
  Industry associations have a major role to play in the development and operation of the markets. They usually have a great deal of influence over the markets and their practice as they are driven by the members of the market but are seen to be an independent body.

- *Issues arising from transacting business in global markets*
  This covers the risks of operating in global markets and includes currency risk, operational risk and personnel risk. Global business often necessitates the use of foreign agents and/or the involvement of international group offices which needs careful consideration and monitoring.

These issues are often complex and yet are of great importance in terms of the managers and supervisor's roles and responsibilities.

The ability of a business to operate safely and effectively in different markets is dependent on operations ability to handle the business efficiently. The service provided by the operations area will be judged by not only the in-house traders, but by the client focussed teams and the client's themselves.

This capability forms part of the overall image and reputation of the organisation.

Managing and supervising an operations team requires adequate managerial knowledge of the markets and products. Team members will be charged with the day-to-day issues of clearing and settlement, however key issues in respect of markets and products must be understood by managers.

These are:

- Market structure and membership rules including liabilities of members
- Products traded
- Structure and characteristics of products
- Clearing mechanisms
- Settlement conventions including conventions applying to underlying assets and associated derivatives
- Structure and role of the Clearing House and Central Securities Depositories
- Clearing membership requirements, rules and regulations including default liabilities
- Client documentation
- Understanding key regulatory and tax issues of the jurisdiction of the market
- Rationale for house and client transactions
- Policy and procedures needed for business on each market and for each product
- Controls needed for business on each market and product.

Without an adequate knowledge of the above it will be impossible for the manager or supervisor to effectively manage the operations team.

We therefore need to look at each of them in greater detail.

MARKET STRUCTURE AND MEMBERSHIP

Exchanges are created or evolve into domestic or international markets. As such each market is different, even when markets are based in the same geographical or legal jurisdiction.

Exchanges are formed to service a perceived need and are structured and sometimes owned accordingly.

Understanding the structure of the market enables the manager to ascertain the benefits and disadvantages of membership of a particular market. It also helps with the choice of Agent to use on a market where, for whatever reason, exchange membership is not deemed appropriate.

Membership of an exchange often allows the manager the opportunity to seek representation on the various committees etc the market may have. This ability to hear about the developments that are planned and to influence thinking and strategy can be of immense importance.

The make up of the membership of a market may be dictated by local regulatory issues. Where this is the case, the manager may need to carefully research the potential counterparts for an agency arrangement or alternatively, manage the requirements for membership by the organisation which may include a local presence, adequately resourced and managed.

This research and the ultimate decision will almost certainly be taken in conjunction with the front office as, depending on the anticipated level of business, it may be prudent from a risk and commercial perspective, for there to be a single counterparty relationship, at least initially.

There will obviously be different criteria for market memberships. Out of these will come operational issues including processing and risk related issues.

An example would be where there is a direct system link such as a transaction matching or registration system. This provides potential advantages in terms of speed and control over transaction processing and monitoring and is also essential for projects like STP mentioned in chapter 1. Membership of the exchange and or clearing house might therefore be more beneficial than an agency arrangement for that market

However exchange membership creates potential liabilities that may or may not be acceptable and so operating on a particular market via an Agent may be more attractive in some circumstances, for instance being an exchange member

PRODUCTS TRADED

As we have already noted understanding the products traded on a market is essentially about the characteristics of the products and the implication for the operational process.

For example, the contract specification for an exchange traded derivative product or the confirmation and associated documentation for securities and other over-the-counter products like derivatives will provide the basic information.

There are however other issues surrounding the products that the operations manager needs to be in possession of.

These include:

- *The impact on the processes and procedures*
  Can the product be incorporated into existing processes and procedures
- System requirements to handle the product
  Is the system able to deal with the product or will there be development work needed
- *Static data control*
  Where and how is the information for the static data to be obtained and how is it to be maintained
- *Regulatory and or exchange reporting requirements*
  What has to be reported, how is the report made and what is the frequency
- *Delivery processes*
  What is the delivery process, timetable and conditions (cash, physical, exchange for physical)
- *Impact of corporate actions or other events*
  How are different corporate actions dealt with, what are the termination or trigger events, what is the "calendar" for the product
- *Control mechanisms for the product*
  What are the risk issues that need addressing

- *Product awareness training for the operations team*
  How are the team to be trained
- *Issues arising from client activity in the product*
  Settlement, collateral, delivery, close outs
- *Funding and collateral issues from activity in products*
  Cashflow, collateral and margin issues
- *Changes to product specifications*
  How notified and what control ensures changes to static data etc are made
- *Introduction of new products*
  Information flow, control to action procedure and static data updates, personnel awareness

All of these must be considered by the managers and supervisors and are important for several reasons including risk management and client service performance. They also have regulatory implications such as whether they are authorised products for certain types of client.

Product knowledge is fundamental for the ability to design procedures, processes and controls, and thus the successful management of a securities, treasury or derivatives operations team.

STRUCTURE AND CHARACTERISTICS OF THE PRODUCTS

Operations teams will all be different such that an operations manager may be dealing with exchange traded products or over-the-counter products or both.

The structure of the products, which will have a major impact on the procedures, processes and controls, vary as do the characteristics.

With the majority of exchange traded products there are core elements to the structure such as number of shares or value of instrument, contract size, settlement date delivery months, tick size and value etc. It is the variables that create the potential for problems and yet these are still relatively easy to manage.

The more exotic the product is, the greater the chance of a non-standard settlement feature, and thus the greater the risk potential.

The manager needs to find the right balance between understanding the key features of a product and the routine processing of that product.

Key Features can be described as:

- Exchange traded or over-the-counter
- Settlement convention
- Registered or bearer
- Delivery terms and conditions
- Funding and capital adequacy requirements
- Regulatory issues.

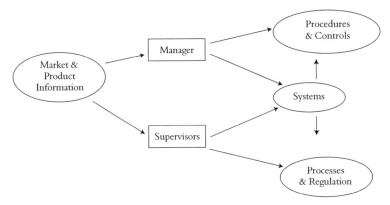

Figure 2.5 Information flow in the operations environment

The above flow diagram illustrates how the manager utilises the market and product information to develop controls and procedures as well as linking this to system development.

At the same time the supervisors will be utilising market and product information for development of suitable processes again linked to system development.

There is so much change currently taking place in the industry that affects markets and exchanges that the manager needs to organise a continuous and comprehensive supply of information in order to keep up with developments.

To recap, the following list shows some of the major changes that have taken place or are taking place:

- Major open out-cry markets switching to electronic trading
- Key derivative and stock exchanges merging
- Derivative and securities clearers expanding product ranges and linking
- Regulation in the UK being centralised into a single regulator
- "New" markets like BrokerTech, JIWAY
- Internet trading and settlement services.

In the rest of the book we look at specific topics and also set out some exercises in the form of work sessions for you to use. The first work session is detailed below. It is suggested that you research background for the session and then relate that to the comments made in this book.

WORK SESSION

Consider the impact and implications for the operations manager of the above changes and developments describing how this will apply short, medium and long term

CLEARING MECHANISMS, MEMBERSHIP AND THE CLEARING HOUSE ROLE

The role of the Clearing House is based on providing services to the exchange that enable the business transacted on that exchange to be settled efficiently and to varying degrees the associated risk managed.

The clearing house achieves this through:

- Acting as the counterparty to each trade
- Calculating the settlement amounts due from all clearing members
- Providing the settlement mechanism including closing out of liabilities
- Managing risk through the setting and collecting of initial margin deposits
- Providing the mechanism for delivery
- Establishing rules and procedures for clearing members
- Establishing default procedures
- Managing a default fund to provide protection to the exchange and its members in the event of a default by a clearing member.

Understanding the clearing mechanism for each exchange is important from the point of view of the settlement processes, "give ups" and timings applicable to delivery. With differences to the procedures on each market the manager must ensure that the supervisors and team are familiar with the various routings, deadlines etc.

Securities and derivatives clearing has traditionally been very different. In securities settlement the counterparty relationship at trade time remains through to settlement. Alternatively, with derivatives, a central clearing counterparty role operates whereby the clearing house becomes the counterparty to the trade. The clearing and settlement process used in derivatives is based on a margin process rather than the full value settlement traditionally used for securities

However a central counterparty process for securities clearing is being and has been introduced in various markets including in London where CREST and The London Clearing House have introduced Equityclear. Similar products have been introduced elsewhere including by Clearnet on the EURONEXT exchanges.

In respect of derivatives efficient margin management, this process also requires an understanding of the acceptable collateral, administration costs of utilising collateral and the relevant client money treatment of assets lodged at the clearing house.

Clearing services such as the London Clearing Houses Equityclear, Swapclear and Repoclear products need to be understood so that the settlement of products through both central clearing and non-central routes can be successfully handled by the team.

It is important to study the appendices that provide an illustration of the way in which the clearing mechanism works for important clearing organisations:

1. CREST and the London Clearing House (including Swapclear)
2. Clearstream
3. Depository Trust & Clearing Corporation.

STRUCTURE OF SECURITIES CLEARING AND SETTLEMENT CONVENTIONS

Although the majority of securities settle in full within a time scale, most exchange traded derivatives never go to delivery. It is a key part of the overall clearing and settlement process that delivery should take place on settlement date. Failure to administer the process correctly will result in fines and reputation damage to the firm.

Therefore the operations manager must concentrate on the processes needed to ensure compliance with the settlement conventions, and when that is not possible, that appropriate escalation procedures and actions monitor, report and control late/failed settlement scenarios. If we bear in mind the cause of the problems with settlement on due date may be caused by counterparties, then we need relevant documenting of costs and losses for possible claims against the errant counterparty.

There is also the matter of collateral that may be utilised, corporate actions and other events that might affect the derivative product either directly or indirectly.

It is therefore important for the operations manager and team to understand the settlement conventions applying for both securities and derivatives products. The manager needs to ensure he and the team have an adequate knowledge of:

- Bond markets
- Equity markets (including Exchange Traded Funds)
- Commodities
- Money markets
- Derivative markets.

An important part of business is client documentation. However in many organisations client documentation is dealt with by a separate department external to the operations team.

It is nevertheless important for the manager to understand the relevant parts of client documentation as clearly there will be times where an operational issue arises and the action will be dictated by the contents and terms of the documentation.

This will apply whether the documentation refers to a client of the firm or to an agent the firm is using ie, the firm is a client. Equally it will apply between fund managers and the client, the client and the custodians, fund managers and custodians and trustees.

In most cases standard documentation is used covering various products. Derivatives agreements may be separate and may also differ between on exchange and off exchange products.

In many cases standardised documentation is now used, an example being that produced by the *International Swaps and Derivatives Association* (ISDA). This is an association which is primarily for participants in the over-the-counter derivatives markets. It aims to promote the development of prudent risk management practices and is a forum for analysis and discussion of issues and developments in the over-the-counter derivatives markets. ISDA set standards for the efficient conduct of business which includes the development and maintenance of derivatives documentation.

In the case of over-the-counter swap transactions, the confirmations supporting the standard ISDA documentation may be dealt with by the operations team. The manager is therefore responsible for ensuring adequate procedures, controls and expertise is available in the team to handle this.

Compliance issues will be referred to throughout the book.

REGULATION, ACCOUNTING AND TAX ISSUES

As with client documentation, the bulk of the work related to regulation and tax is likely to be handled elsewhere in the firm. Nevertheless there will be issues that impact on the operations function and have implications for the manager.

Ensuring that the firm is complying with the relevant rules and regulations in each market place and jurisdiction is a joint effort by the compliance officer and the operations manager.

Regulation is dealt with elsewhere in the book but as a "product" it is clear that the manager must have more than a passing knowledge of the subject and also ensure that supervisors and staff understand reasons for, and the importance of, regulation.

Likewise accounting and tax implications in terms of realised and unrealised profit / losses, hedge trades, utilising collateral, withholding tax , assets delivery arising from derivatives etc. need to be understood.

Ensuring that the firm meets industry standards and regulatory requirements over valuations and reporting of assets under management, including performance, is also important.

POLICY, PROCEDURES AND CONTROLS

Central to the successful management of an operations team is the policy introduced by the manager covering procedures and controls.

The core element of delivery of the policy is the knowledge and understanding of the markets and products that the operations team process.

The more complex and diverse the business activity, the greater the need for a manager to comprehend the background environment of the transactions.

This means understanding the:

- Rationale for the types of transactions that take place
- Characteristics of the products used
- Exchange and clearing issues
- Implications in terms of controls, regulation and risk
- System requirements to handle the transaction and or product
- Overview of the settlement process.

These headings are of course then subject to further sub-headings as the more detailed analysis occurs. These are covered at various stages in the book and further information and sources of information is provided in the appendices.

In this chapter of the book we have looked at the importance of market and product knowledge as part of the managers role. The ability to successfully manage the operations team stems largely from the respect the personnel have for the manager.

This includes the manager's ability to comprehend the problems and introduce effective solutions as well as the skill in leaving processing and day-to-day issues to the supervisors whilst clearly being capable of dealing with the higher level issues.

Market and product knowledge is the key to a manager instilling the confidence into the team and earning their respect.

WORK SESSION

Consider the key procedures and controls that will be necessary for a transaction in:

- **A UK equity transaction in ordinary shares and an equity option on the same stock**
- **A US treasury bond and associated CBOT Bond futures contract**
- **A Eurex equity stock option**
- **A London Metal Exchange Copper contract**
- **An interest rate swap**

3

BANKING, BROKING AND INSTITUTIONAL CLIENTS

Within the financial markets the roles of banking, broking and fund management are relatively simple concepts. Today these functions are often combined in global investment banks and thus we have multi-product firms as well as specialist or niche firms.

The business profile of each is important to understand for the majority of operations managers for the simple reason that relationships on a client or principal basis will almost certainly exist between different organisations. It is therefore essential to know how these counterparties operate, what issues they face and how this will impact both positively and negatively.

Banking, investment and merchant, is no longer a business defined along rigid lines. Today a bank can have a broking capacity, a fund management capacity a merchant banking arm and a retail banking function. We can see this with the likes of Prudential and Egg, and Standard Life and its mortgage bank. Other examples are Merrill Lynch and its asset management arm and Barclays Bank retail banking and broking business. In fact the "specialist" firm is getting difficult to find with even small private client brokers being linked to larger organisations.

The internet has also changed the structure in financial markets with many "broking" firms setting up operations to meet the demands of the "new" private client!

The global investment bank as we know has evolved from the removal or loosening of the regulatory environment governing participants in the financial markets. This allowed external or foreign entities to acquire stakes in banks, brokers and fund management companies in both domestic and other countries.

However global investment banks have not been structured identically. We have organisations that are controlled out of a central hub and these types of firm will inevitably have a high degree of uniform systems, procedures and practices, coupled with client facing services designed to be in a universal corporate style. Controls will be centrally administered and this will apply across the front office and support areas including operations. Staffing will be "group-wide" with many different nationalities working in the offices around the world.

Other organisations have adopted a more regional approach allowing much of the management of the firm to be somewhat autonomous with only certain activities such as systems centralised. Client services are tailored, local practices recognised and decision making largely left to the managers.

In scenario one the banks will be looking at their global corporate clients, whilst at the same time seeking to provide a localised broking service to key domestic clients. Fund management arms may be driven from the central location or may be at arms length, working on and building from the strength of name, market awareness, investor profile etc.

The benefits of uniformity in scenario one would be development and ease of distribution of global products and services, cost savings, marketing profile, interchangability of staff, systems etc. and the central risk control. Downside issues will be the "global" product versus a "localised" delivery of the product, referrals for decisions and difficulties in maintaining an even standard across the offices world-wide.

In scenario two the benefits are primarily the concentration on developing and servicing local clients in domestic products with an option to offer a global service by networking the various centres of the firm. The individual strengths of the various offices in theory are then utilised to provide a strong global product to the client base that wants it.

The downside is the difficulty in actually providing this as well as significant concerns about the ability to maintain satisfactory levels of risk management when so much decision making and procedures are vested in local managers.

It is not possible to say that one or other, or the many variations, is the right way to establish a global business as clearly each route has its merits and deficiencies. If you are currently employed in such an organisation you will be aware of the kind of problems that occur.

Also the business profile is key here. If a firm offers Prime Brokerage or Global Clearing in derivatives for instance, a truly integrated operations function globally is essential to the successful delivery of the service. Prime Brokerage and Global Clearing in derivatives are both services provided by banks and brokers that offer benefits to the client in the form of reducing the number of counterparties for dealing and or settlement, enabling efficiencies in cost and administration and providing access to value-added services based on technology, funding, stock lending/borrowing, reporting etc.

Equally when we look at fund management companies there is likely to be a situation where the company may administer domestic and international funds from a single location whilst retailing them through sales arms in different locations. Alternatively, funds may be administered and sold in various geographical locations with some kind of central investment policy overlaying the process. Also with fund management, the firm appointed as custodian for the safekeeping of assets etc. may be appointed by the fund managers or by the client on whose behalf the manager operates.

Quite often a UK based fund manager may well have offices in, for instance, Boston USA and Hong Kong which will service certain local clients and deliver products for the local market. These operations may be significantly smaller than the UK operation.

As far as the settlement and administration processes go, the UK operations manager may have responsibility for these offices and any staff working there.

WHAT ARE THE ISSUES FOR THE OPERATIONS MANAGERS IN THESE SCENARIOS?

Perhaps the first and most important is the lines of reporting and communication. Consider the following diagram giving a global structure for a firm:

Example Global Structure

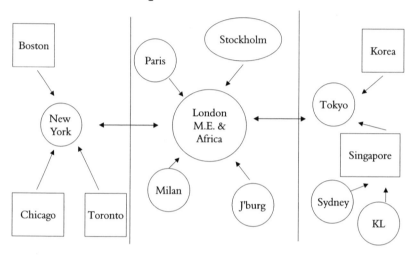

Figure 3.1

Whatever the specific structure, there is always the need for data to flow back and forth between centres in addition to that which flows between the centre and its various counterparts. As the diagram shows, the three hub principle allows the operations function to flow around the world, around the clock. In theory a global client can access any market or transaction and settlement data 24 hours a day from any of its locations.

The following diagram illustrates just some of the potential relationships that an operations team has.

Operations Internal Relationships

Operations External Relationships

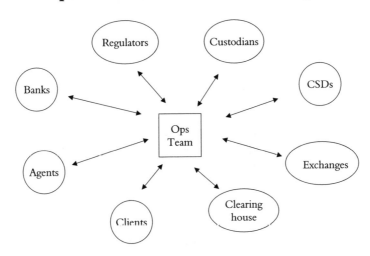

Figure 3.2

With so many local relationships to manage in addition to the inter-hub relationship, it is not difficult to see just how highly skilled the managers and staff need to operate within such a structure. As straight through processing, central clearing and dematerialised settlement become the standard in most major markets, the difficulties experienced by firms operating global operations functions will change.

In addition to reliable, fast data flow and effective communication, there are problems such as risk management, staff competency, the impact different types of client have on the workflow processes etc.

When we look at risk later in the book it will easy to see just how the risk profile of global operations is different from that of operations functions dealing with local markets.

But what of the smaller organisations that are not "global" in presence but nevertheless operate in global markets? What are the problems for operations managers here?

Essentially they are the same ie, communication and data flow through the agents being used to provide access to global markets.

But obviously the operations profile of a private client broker is going to be quite different from a global investment bank and yet the problems whilst different in "size" and style, are very similar for the manager.

Poor systems or lack of competent staff will impact as severely, maybe significantly more severely in a small broker or fund manager as they possibly would in Morgan Stanley Dean Witter or Deutsche Bank.

As the cost of providing complex systems and resource is high, organisations such as private client stockbrokers will often outsource their client settlement etc. to agents that have the skills and infrastructure to deliver services and manage client assets and money.

Within the exchange traded derivatives arena fund managers, and small medium size clients will utilise global or centralised clearing facilities offered by larger banks to remove the responsibilities of settling obligations with the clearing house of the market and also streamlining the settlement process to a single counterparty.

For major banks such as UBS Warburg, the global clearing services in exchange traded derivatives is an important business being as it is a part of a portfolio of services and products offered to their clients by the Group.

Managers failing to be aware of developments in the markets, regulation or clearing and settlement environments are as a big a liability in the global fund manager as they are in a small domestic fund management company.

It is therefore very important for an operations manager to not only understand the business of their own firm and the functions of operations teams within the firm, but also how other firms are structured.

The facilities and services on offer to fund management companies through banks, CSDs and custodians, if utilised effectively, will save money and reduce risk, both of which are fundamental objectives of operations managers!

This principle therefore also applies to the staff in the operations team, particularly those dealing directly with other firms be they banks, agents, suppliers or clients.

It makes good sense to not only train staff for the role they undertake internally but also to train them in the other areas of the industry that affect them directly and indirectly.

Suggested courses and further reading are provided in the Appendices.

WORK SESSION

Consider the clearing, settlement and risk issues for a broker with both fund management and private clients that are operating in international markets.

4

CONCEPTS OF RISK

Operational Risk is a major issue for the operations manager and in this chapter we explore the subject and the way in which operational, market and credit risk impact.

The whole subject of risk is not new and yet in reality operational risk was certainly not so high on the agenda until high profile problems and losses, as a result of operational in efficiency started to materialise. For managers, some aspects of operational risk such as settlement risk, are part of the day-to-day workflow and are managed accordingly. Efficiency in the operations team is therefore an element of the management of one part of operational risk at least in that efficient settlement reduces settlement risk. However, we also need to remember that our performance levels may not be reflected in the performance of agents and counterparties we deal with so we are exposed to a counterparty risk element of operational risk. There are other examples of risk which we will look at in a moment but it is clear that operational risk is in two parts, that which we generate and control and that which is generated from external sources and needs controlling. For instance, errors and inefficiency in trade input for principal trading are internally generated problems whereas inefficiency in a custody provided are externally generated. One may be tempted to think that the external risk issues are more difficult to deal with but this may not be the case. Dealing with internal resource issues can be more demanding than using service level agreements to raise the performance of an external counterparty.

The subject of operational risk raises several key issues. These include:

- The approach to risk
- The sources of risk
- The impact of risk
- Measuring risk including the cost of managing risk
- Introducing controls and procedures
- Why disasters will happen if it is not managed.

Operational risk and operations risk are not new concepts, as we have said. As soon as the first ever trade took place operational risk came into being and yet it is only comparatively recently that there has been an acceptance that operational risk exists. Contrast this with market and credit risk, both of which have been recognised since the 1970s. Defining risk is a little subjective especially when we talk about operational risk. Below are definitions;

DEFINITIONS

Market Risk can be described as the risk of financial loss due to trading errors, adverse market movements or breaches of market rules and regulations.

Credit Risk can be described as the risk of financial loss due to the likelihood of a failure by a counterparty.

Operational Risk is defined by the Risk Management Group of the Basel Committee as "the risk of loss resulting from inadequate or failed internal processes, people and systems or from external events".

It could also, and is, described as everything that is not or does not fall into market or credit risk.

The Basel Committee was formed in 1974 by the central-bank Governors of the Group of Ten countries and it has approximately thirty technical working groups which meet regularly. It is part of the Bank for International Settlements (BIS). Its recommendations do not have any legal force but are intended to bring about common standards and practices amongst its members' systems. One of its important objectives is to ensure that no foreign banking establishment is without adequate supervision. In 1997 the Committee developed a set of "Core Principles for Effective Banking Supervision". Further to this in 1999, it published the "Core Principles Methodology" to assist in the implementation and assessment of the Principles.

Both market and credit risk have been high on the agenda of regulators and risk managers. An example is perhaps the capital adequacy requirements pertaining to over-the-counter derivative transactions. The Basel Committee has been looking at the subject for some years now and has through the Basel Accord and the New Basel Accord (published January 2001) provided a proposed framework for the regulatory capital charge for operational risk. In outlining proposals for the development of a capital charge to cover operational risk the committee has set out three approaches of increasing sophistication to assessing the operational risk charge. These are *The Basic Indicator Charge*, the *Standardised Approach* and the *Internal Measurement Approach*. These proposals are subject to surveys and data collection by the Committee and it is important to remain up to date with developments. For this reason I do not propose to put into this chapter details of the Accords or papers given that change is taking place and instead suggest the following work session is undertaken

WORK SESSION

There are many papers and other information published by the BIS and these are available on their website <u>www.bis.org</u>

From the website study the proposals and amendments as they are being published and consider how these will impact on your organisation and on the operations team.

Whilst BIS has set out definitions of operational risk I find in my dealings with clients on this matter that there is still the issue of defining operational risk in terms of the day-to-day workflow. What really is Operational Risk? Well, one reason for the delay in recognising operational risk is that as a category of risk it is probably the most difficult to determine and even Basel recognises that some of the parameters in their risk assessment overlap with market and credit risk so once again, we ask the question - what exactly is operational risk!

As we have seen in the definitions, some would argue that it is everything that affects a business that is not market or credit risk. Others argue that it is everything and anything to do with the post transaction clearing and settlement process. In the case of the latter, the risk itself is described as "operations" rather than operational risk. For the purposes of this book we will consider operational risk as being anything that is not market or credit risk. That said, we may find that the views expressed in this book are not the same views taken by risk managers in different organisations. Also some organisations have been focussing on operational risk for many years and have refined their assessment of it. There are many different approaches to risk in the industry today, but of course the regulatory requirements concerning risk are vitally important to understand. Both domestic regulators and international organisations will have risk related regulation and recommendations that firms will adhere to. In addition to the regulatory situation we also have recommendations from organisations such as ISSA that are designed to improve efficiency and reduce settlement, systems and counterparty risk.

Equally, firms will need to have a risk strategy that applies to their particular business and which they are comfortable with. No two firms have identical approaches to risk, although as noted, some risk management requirement is mandatory. Another key factor is that many view the subject of risk primarily in terms of potential financial loss. As such operational risk is frequently considered to be unlikely to cause a severe financial loss and certainly not in one hit. The logic here is that an inappropriate or incorrect deal can result in substantial loss, whereas a settlement problem with the transaction, whilst it may incur costs, is not likely to generate a significant loss.

One is tempted initially to agree with these sentiments as history would tend to suggest that the headline making "disasters" in the financial services industry are all mainly related to Market and or Credit risk. However delve a little deeper and there may be associated operations issues that contributed to the problem. The contribution may not have been "physical" in the sense of an error in processing transactions, but rather a failure to carry out the risk management role that operations undoubtedly have. Basel also recognise this and note that some risks and loss events previously recorded as credit or market risk may actually sit in operational risk, or indeed in more than one category. It is also worth noting at this point that the current proposed framework for a capital charge ignores systemic risk and therefore it has been sated that the charge would need to be calibrated to reflect this.

It is important to consider how the manifestation of operational risk occurs because in my experience it is not always an up front or visible scenario. Operational risk can manifest itself in many ways. Sometimes the operational risk will be such that it is not easily or immediately identifiable. In most cases an error on a transaction can and should be identified quickly and adjusted so that the loss is quantified. With operations for instance, a problem may be occurring only occasionally and yet is having an unseen, dramatic and damaging effect. For instance, a client is being inconvenienced by occasional late and error strewn reports and settlement and as such, is losing confidence in the broker/bank as their counterparty. In such a situation it is not inconceivable that the client may gradually move their business elsewhere and the counterparty may never be aware that it is the operations teams performance that is to blame.

Equally we need to consider how to quantify and measure operational risk.

Typical ways of measuring risk relate to the allocating of capital against potential losses based for instance on *Value at Risk* (VaR), historical losses attributable to risk situations and exposures, for instance credit ratings. This is not too difficult when we look at market and credit risk measurement and management

Operational risk however is difficult to measure and hard to quantify in terms of likely financial loss. It is therefore difficult to allocate capital to cover such a risk turning into an actual loss.

The establishing of the extent of the market risk associated with trading is not simple but it is nevertheless possible to measure the exposure given various scenarios and to allocate capital to cover the possible worst-case outcome. Value at Risk is one common approach, but it is less easy to apply this when dealing with operational risk although a *Value at Operational Risk* (VaOR) and other technical methodology has been worked on extensively in the industry to find ways of quantifying operational risk. Nevertheless, despite this progress being made on operational risk models as more and more organisations seek to quantify the operational risk of their business, there are still many operational risk management processes that rely on subjective assessment and input. It is therefore important that managers begin the process of measuring risk by developing both subjective monitoring of elements that contribute to operational risk sources as well as researching the risk measurement models used in-house or likely to be used.

For the day-to-day risk management process, what would we need to incorporate into operational risk measurement? When we look at quantifying and measuring operational risk we need to first consider what it consists of.

At high level, operational risk can be said to comprise:

- Settlement Risk
- System Risk
- Personnel Risk
- Infrastructure Risk
- Counterparty Risk
- Regulatory Risk
- Legal risk
- Reputational Risk.

These risks are fully explained later in the chapter.

However within these headings are many sub-sets of risk that can and often do combine to generate risk situations that go across one or more categories. A significant danger therefore is combinations of risks. The combination of risks makes measuring and managing operational risk a complex exercise and indeed it can also result in the situation where the cost of managing the risk is prohibitive. As with all types of risk, there is operational risk that is acceptable as part of the business, provided that the risk is known and understood. There is a danger that the subject of operational risk can be so diverse and so large that it becomes an administrative and costly nightmare. It is therefore important for any organisation and any individual manager with responsibility for operational risk to establish exactly what the objectives are when we talk about measuring and managing operational risk.

One approach for the operations manager to take is to consider risk statements and then analyse them firstly in terms of the particular operational function they are involved with and then for other operational areas of the firm and counterparts.

Consider the following statements, which will help us to analyse and define our risk objectives are:

1. Operational risk exists in all businesses
2. We can ascertain what operational risk is in the context of our business
3. We can look at individual components of the risk
4. We can choose to be:
   - Aware of the risk

- ○ To be aware of the risk and prioritise managing some of it
- ○ To manage the risk out of the business
5. We may need to adopt a mix and match approach
6. We may need to demonstrate how we manage operational risk:
   - ○ To clients or potential clients
   - ○ To third parties such as clearing houses
   - ○ To regulators
7. We will have to establish a risk culture within the organisation
8. We need to analyse risk in conjunction with:
   - ○ Other parts of the organisation
   - ○ External counterparties
   - ○ Across products and markets
9. We will need to allocate capital in accordance with Basel and internal policy to mitigate against the impact of the operational risk manifesting itself and totally ignoring operational risk is not an option.

When looking at an operational risk model we need to be able to measure risk in such a way that we can:

- Predict the type of risk
- Where, when and how it will arise
- The frequency with which it might occur
- The impact.

There are a variety of ways in which this can be done. One example is by carrying out a process of workflow analysis that will show:

- The processes and their duration
- The complexity, ranking (in terms of primary, secondary) and the extent of automation of these processes
- The deadlines associated with the processes
- The level of resource available for the process
- The level of management needed
- The scope to absorb additional workload and or delays to the processing.

Workflow analysis is discussed at various times in the book but from the above we can see that operational risk measurement is both possible as well as a continuous process.

However when the concept of operational risk needs to be explained to the staff and their buy-in sought to implement change(as indeed when the business managers are approached to get their buy-in to the cost of establishing effective operational risk management) the manager will probably encounter resistance. This is not surprising and it occurs all the time anyway simply because change does not sit comfortably with many people. One possible way to overcome this is to relate the argument to an everyday scenario such as "operational risk may not appear to be an important issue and it may never create a major problem so why all the fuss, but then you could leave your house unlocked all day and never get burgled, do you want to take the risk?"

Having established that operational risk exists and needs to quantified and measured, we need to identify the risk in more detail. We will do this later in the chapter but first let us look at where the risk might come from. Sources of operational risk can be both obvious and sometimes not so obvious.

Here are just a few potential sources:

- Lack of product knowledge
- Poor system reliability
- Inadequate levels of staffing
- Inefficient counterparties
- Diverse and unpredictable business levels
- Overseas clients
- Lack of critical skill sets
- Fraud and criminal activities
- Poor communication and poor internal relationships.

Then we need to consider the type and frequency of risk. Each of these sources is very different and so are the types of risk and the frequency with which they might occur.

For instance lack of product knowledge could be as a result of:

- Turnover of staff
- Loss of experienced personnel
- New products being traded
- Non availability of information
- Lack of training.

It may be a major problem or it may only be relevant if and when a particular type of product is traded. Bear in mind also that other risks may become associated such as regulatory risk and reputational risk. For example a clearing member of a clearing house will usually have to demonstrate the competency of the staff, systems and processes. If problems occur within the members operations function because of the introduction of a new type of product, the clearing house may feel that the member is failing to meet the standards required and any prolonged problem or subsequent repetition may result in the clearing status being withdrawn. The significance of that should not need explaining.

A problem might manifest itself as an error caused because we were not aware of something like a corporate action, expiry date of a derivative, or maturity of a bond or because we were unaware of problems with settlement in the jurisdiction where the product was traded. Some of the problems may be quite obvious, others more obscure. Individually the problem might be easily identified and managed but a combination of risk problems might create a far more difficult situation to manage.

I think we have established that the role of operations managers and their teams in managing risk is a key one. Throughout the book we look at how to manage the risk, but as managers we will have already worked out that much of what we do in an operational environment or an operations team day in day out is geared to directly or indirectly managing risk. A major issue that arises is that the personnel involved in the operations team may not be aware of the importance of their role. Perversely, that in itself is a source of risk!

At this stage we can perhaps summarise operational risk. It is a combination of types and sources of risk that may have a different impact in various circumstances. It may result in direct or indirect financial loss. It may occur frequently or occasionally. It may build up gradually until it is a major problem. It is a risk category of immense importance and must be understood in any organisation large or small. It can be hard to measure but nevertheless must be addressed so that, at the very least, managers are aware of the risks. Failure to understand and address operational risk will result in significant damage to the business. We know that operational risk comes in a variety of guises and that we can breakdown operational risk into several headings. Within each heading will be a complex matrix of possibilities and sources of the risk type.

Let us look at these in more detail:

SETTLEMENT RISK

Definition: *The risk of inefficient processes and procedures resulting in the failure, delay or incorrect settlement of transactions and associated actions such as payments, delivery and corporate actions.*

There are many ways in which this type of risk can occur. The simple inefficiencies of the staff involved are an obvious source. So too is inadequate or misused systems. However not all settlement risk is created within the operations team. External influences such as delays in getting relevant information from front office to operations or problems with systems run on a bureau basis can be very influential.

Other causes of settlement risk are:

- Client transactions
- Deadlines
- Difficult settlement conventions
- Illiquid stocks/bonds/commodities
- Lack of knowledge of the product/processes/procedures associated with the transaction.

SYSTEM RISK

Definition: *The failure of or absence of adequate systems to handle the type of business being transacted and security over such systems, as well as a failure by managers, operations staff, IT staff and others to understand the scope and limitations of the systems and the related workflow.*

The reliance on systems in the financial services industry makes system risk a key issue. STP is a prime example. The advent of straight through processing is removing elements of settlement risk associated with trade input. Electronic markets, internal dealing systems and direct trade input enable the operations team to maximise auto reconciliation and concentrate on exception management. However not all organisations have straight through processing, or if they do it is not necessarily fully front to back. Whatever the situation, the managers must recognise that systems generate considerable capacity, provide efficient and cost effective processing and those systems are also a major source of operational risk.

System security is a key issue. The security over the system is paramount. All too often there are serious problems generated by the failure of managers to adequately manage systems. There are a whole host of possible situations including:

- Incorrect, missing or erroneously changed static data
- Failure to make change contract specification
- Ignored, lack off or breached security of access to the system or parts of the system
- "Shared" passwords lead to breach of segregation
- Access to confidential client information gained by front office
- Inadequate or absence of monitoring of client facing technology services
- Lack of or easily breached firewalls
- Lack or absence of control over access to internet
- Private, illegal or unauthorised access, download etc
- Possibility of hackers and or viruses entering the system.

System capability and reliability is another key area. It is fairly obvious that any system used in any operations environment needs to be able to adequately handle the products traded. Where this is not possible as might be the case with use of over-the-counter derivatives, controls need to be devised which will mitigate the risk. End-user organisations can have problems verifying margin calls on the systems they use and managers need to address this issue with suitable controls encompassing the reasonableness of the calls. In terms of reliability, there needs to be awareness of:

- The manual process that can/will be implemented
- The impact this will have on the risk exposure
- The procedures and controls that will now apply
- The potential solutions to eradicate the unreliability.

COUNTERPARTY AND AGENT RISK

Counterparty risk is not confined to credit worthiness. The performance of a counterparty can have a material effect on the operations team. Where it is necessary to use an agent, for instance an institutional client using a broker or a broker/bank using a clearing agent on an exchange where they do not have clearing membership, there is potential for heightened operational risk. The standards of performance by these agents will inevitably impact upon the processes and performance of our own team.

Late settlement, notification, or payment are all significant and may have far reaching implications.

Issues that arise are:

- Regulatory
- Reputation
- Client money and assets policy
- Increased costs.

Similar kinds of issues arise in respect of clients. We are dependent on the accurate and timely flow of information concerning transactions, payments, booking instructions etc. If a position is to go to delivery the broker/bank is dependent on the client meeting the delivery schedule and deadlines or they may become liable.

In some cases, there may be very limited resource and product knowledge at the client and the potential for problems is increased. In many cases, the broker/bank may also be dealing with a custodian. Broker/banks also offer a wide range of client services which may include:

- Prime Brokerage
- Global clearing
- Single currency settlement
- Average pricing
- Custody.

Each of these is placing additional pressures on the operations processing flow and therefore whilst it can be said that client services help to reduce counterparty risk (by providing vital assistance to smooth the settlement flow), its provision does create additional sources of risk internally.

PERSONNEL RISK

Key issues that arise under this source of risk include:

- Fraud
- Defections/loss of senior staff
- Lack of contingency for absence of staff

- Inadequate training and development
- Relationship issues (work and private)
- Excessive pressure caused by poor working environment and hours.

Personnel Risk has several key issues.

Knowledge and Competency
The knowledge and expertise of staff in all areas is crucial to a business's success. However, this expertise needs to be relevant and current in order to meet the demands and ever-changing financial industry. It is vitally important that a company demonstrates a commitment to staff training programmes and constant staff development. The quality and integrity of managers and supervisors in an operations environment should be considered and whilst a turnover of staff is to be expected, this turnover should be small and monitored.

Staff Turnover
Where personnel turnover is constant, in any area of the business, then questions should be raised about the reasons for this and the effect that it is having on the business should be monitored. However, the future effect that it may have cannot easily be measured but could potentially be disastrous!

Processing
Within personnel risk, there is an element of danger associated with routine and possibly monotonous tasks. Managers and supervisors should monitor this and, where possible, staff should be rotated or cross-trained to avoid this situation. Mistakes can be made and errors may not be detected where staff are not paying full attention to their tasks due to the repetitive nature. As part of straight through processing (STP) projects, these types of tasks should be reviewed and where possible will be automated.

Management Style
Whilst managers and supervisors need to instil discipline in their staff and their practices, this needs to be carefully managed so as not to create an atmosphere of fear of making mistakes and a fear of owning up to them. This will lead to covering up and can lead to more errors, which occur due to the cover up. In reality, there will be mistakes and staff need to be open about admitting to them. Given the pressures, the so called open door or approachable management style is crucially important in today's operational environment.

Relationships

An element of personnel risk which needs to be controlled and managed properly is the front/back office relationship. There needs to be mutual respect for each other's roles and there should be good communication channels in order to efficiently resolve problems and errors that occur. However, if the relationship is too close, then that is a potential danger due to the possibility of fraud.

The way in which personnel interact with clients and counterparties is important. Where staff are directly involved with clients and other counterparties, then they should be trained in how to deal with them. This includes more simple matters such as the way in which they speak to outside people to what they should/shouldn't tell them. Choosing the right people with good communication skills for these roles is vital as primarily they represent the company to the outside world.

The issue of personnel risk is often ignored, yet the efficiency and effectiveness of the operations team, which is key to profitability, is directly related to the managers ability to develop the right people and the right environment which in turn is at the heart of operational risk management. Lack of attention to personnel risk will, sooner or later, create a major problem, as other risk control measures are dependent upon and assume a "risk culture" has been established in the team.

REGULATORY RISK

It is often tempting to ignore regulatory risk on the misguided assumption that compliance and or audit will protect against any problem. To some extent they do, but operations influences regulatory risk as it often generates data used in regulatory reporting and also is in the front line in areas such as client money and assets. Recognising regulatory risk as part of operational risk is essential simply because the consequences of not doing so is too great.

- Regulatory risk stems from several sources including:
- Reporting requirements
- Client money rules
- Money laundering and fraud (insider dealing)
- Complex and differing requirements in regulatory jurisdictions
- Reputational impact of a breach of regulation.

LEGAL RISK

As with regulation, it is tempting to say that legal issues are dealt with elsewhere in the organisation. However there are many instances where operations personnel are either directly or indirectly involved with matters that present an operational risk.

These will include:

- Ineffective, absence of or incorrect client documentation in respect of:
  - OTC derivative transactions
  - The seizing or impounding of assets
  - Entering into illegal transactions or relationships or carrying out actions/instructions that would be considered illegal

REPUTATIONAL RISK

This is the importance of the way in which your company is perceived to the outside world. It can be damaged in the ways in which we have looked at under personnel risk. It can also be damaged by inadequate controls over the business, which can lead to a bad reputation in the market. Reputational risk is not confined to client business, it can also affect your relationship with counterparties. This can be damaged if you do not settle efficiently and operate properly with counterparties. You may be at risk from clients and counterparties damaging your reputation and therefore you must have strict procedures for operating with third parties and must take action when they put your business reputation at risk.

INFRASTRUCTURE RISK

There is a significant operational risk in having an ineffective or inappropriate infrastructure to handle the business of the firm. As changes impact on the industry as a whole, so the infrastructures within organisations need to change. Procedures, processes, reporting lines, departments/sections, roles and functions can and will need reviewing and adapting. A failure to do this will lead to unnecessary pressures on people and systems, higher error rates, lack of capacity to handle growth and almost certainly higher costs to the business.

FINANCIAL RISK

Some elements of financial risk could be classified as settlement risk. This might include errors resulting in interest claims or fines for late delivery for instance. However financial risk does exist in other forms as part operational risk.

Included in this would be:

- Fraud and default
- Ineffective costs management
- Unclaimed and/or unreconciled floor brokerage
- Poor treasury management.

These are areas that are often "lost" in the overall process of running an operations team. Costs management for instance may be an issue when business is slow, but is relaxed when revenues and profits are good. Likewise significant additional costs or underperformance of returns on invested capital occur if treasury management is neglected or is carried out by inadequately trained personnel. It may not be significant on a day-by-day basis but the cumulative effect over a year can be very significant.

DISASTER RISK

This broadly constitutes the inability to, or reduced ability continue to operate and can cover such areas as:

- Inadequate disaster recovery or business continuation plans
- Forcing of a curtailment or reduction in trading levels
- Unacceptable risk situations.

Many organisations have adequate contingency plans for disasters such as loss of premises. From an operations point of view, there are many possible disaster situations that have nothing to do with the loss of the premises. Some of these would be:

- Sudden unavailability of staff
- Prolonged system downtime
- External factors such as problems at agents, clearing houses, clients
- Breaches of client confidentiality.

In this chapter of the book we have looked at an overview of operational risk. We have considered what it is, where it comes from and how it occurs.

We have looked at simplistic ways in which this risk can be measured and at some of the key issues that will need to be managed.

Operational risk is a vital element that needs to be considered by any business operating in financial markets and products. It is a large and diverse subject that needs careful assessment, interpretation of its characteristics in relation to each organisation and, above all, managing.

We can therefore conclude that the manager's role in operational risk management is a crucial one so what are the key points in terms of managing the risk and fulfilling the role and responsibilities?

First and foremost is the manager's own understanding of the risk issues, the ways in which their organisation is already addressing the risk issues and the general risk culture that currently exists within the organisation and the operations team. Once this assessment is completed, we can look at tools to help the management process and provide the input to the risk management process in the firm. We have already seen how workflow analysis provides the key efficiency indicators and where possible the use of benchmarks should also be used. Then we need to consider the risk awareness of the team and ensure that adequate training is provided to bring the level of awareness and buy-in to the required status.

Procedures, including those related to risk sources and management, need to be documented and constantly reviewed and updated as the risk environment changes constantly. Particular care must be taken to ensure that the procedures reflect regulatory changes, industry rationalisations, industry best practices and of course internal changes to business profiles, structures etc. Given that we are talking about global operations management, this process needs to be completed for each jurisdiction, market etc. The operations manager needs their own "strategy" to monitor the risks, the sources, the controls and the effectiveness of the controls.

Any risk situations that do materialise need to be logged, actions taken and or referred to the risk manager or group and then monitored. Any financial cost ie, claims, losses also need to be logged and, if appropriate, reported to the risk manager for the loss database (loss database will have been covered in your BIS/Basel works session earlier in this chapter). The management information in current use for general purposes can often be adapted and utilised for operational risk management information purposes.

If, from the management information (MI) data and from other sources ie, supervisors views etc, there are significant risk scenarios or sources arising then the manager must take action. This would include risks generated by system issues, resourcing, working environment, counterparty/agent, and the action will range from re-engineering operations teams to replacing a counterparty.

Operational risk management should be very much pro-active rather than reactive management. Planning and assessing are key tools in managing the risk before rather than after it happens. Of course the unexpected always will occur and then the speed of and appropriateness of the course of action will be imperative.

Sources of operational risk are diverse so in the rest of the book when we look at specific functions, processes and procedures it is logical to do so from the risk point of view as well.

Organisations have different approaches to managing risk. The following four diagrams illustrate how the management of risk might be structured.

Figure 4.1 shows the approach of day to day risk being managed as part of the workflow and responsibilities of the supervisors and operations team with the operations manager overseeing the control and liaising with the risk manager. This approach to operational risks is replicated through the organisation, covering different departments and or sections. The risk manager is therefore receiving data and discussing issues and actions with the manager on the basis of exceptions to the risk limits and profiles set for the area concerned.

Operational Risk

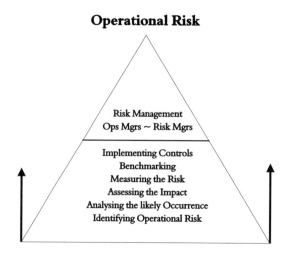

Figure 4.1

Figure 4.2 shows the extension of this approach to illustrate the general roles of the operations and risk managers and that of the Board. The Board will react to the reports from the risk manager which will include recommendations and requirements for resource, policy changes etc.

Operational Risk Structure

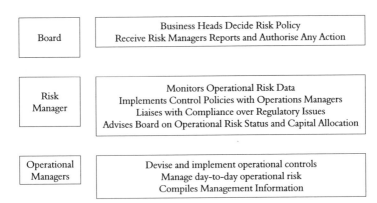

Figure 4.2

Figure 4.3 shows how the measurement of operational risk might be incorporated into a model. The risk approach and identified sources of risk are mapped into the workflow and resulting management information is used to develop controls. The controls are monitored to give the effectiveness of the risk management and to provide historic and predicted potential occurrences of different risks, including the severity if it were to occur. Against this, capital can be set aside according to the organisations risk view and policy and any regulatory requirements.

Operational Risk Model - 1

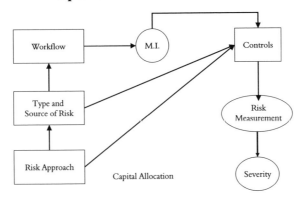

Figure 4.3

Figure 4.4 shows additional sources of input to the control process so that any accounting, regulatory, or industry best practices etc can be incorporated into the risk standard to be used.

Operational Risk Model 1a

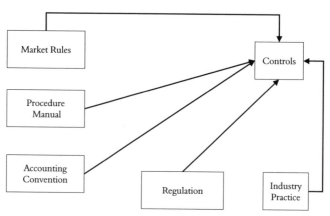

Figure 4.4

Managing operational and operations risk is still in essence about the efficiency and effectiveness of the managers, supervisors and staff. Models can show what might happen and predict financial losses, but the people are both a key source of risk and the strongest way to manage it.

There are many articles and books that deal with operations and operational risk as well as papers published by for instance, ISSA and BIS (see appendices). Despite the fact that there are core risks that affect all organisations, the type and degree of impact of operational and operations risk will vary from business to business and organisation to organisation. Consider the types of risk categories that are likely to apply to your organisation and assess the ways in which that risk is identified and managed.

5

CLEARING AND SETTLEMENT

In this chapter we are going to look at the clearing and settlement processes in some detail, but clearing and settlement takes place after the transaction, although there are, as we will see, certain processes that operations are involved in prior to trades taking place.

Trading in securities, whether in the *Exchange Traded* (sometimes referred to as the *regulated* markets) or the *Over The Counter* (OTC) markets, generally takes place by telephone or through electronic dealing systems. With most securities once a trade is executed, both parties to the trade enter into a legally binding obligation or agreement that commits them to make a delivery of securities from the seller to the buyer in return for the equivalent value in cash. Derivatives are slightly different as with some types of products, for instance purchasing options the trade is for a right to do something and not an obligation.

There are essentially three stages in clearing and settlement:

- Pre-settlement
- Settlement
- Post-settlement.

The first task in the pre-settlement phase is to ensure that both counterparties recognise that the details of a particular trade are consistent. This is achieved by the exchange of confirmations, which enables one counterparty to allow the other to check all the trade details against its records. As settlement cycles are shortening, counterparties need to exchange their confirmations more rapidly. The traditional methods of sending paper contract notes and telex confirmations transaction confirmations are no longer appropriate and alternative media include *Electronic Trade Confirmation* (ETC) and SWIFT messages.

It is necessary to perform a prompt confirmation-checking routine so that any problems that arise can be resolved as soon as possible (or within pre-determined deadlines set by the market). Trades that are un-confirmed for whatever reason cannot proceed to the settlement stage. It is important to note that the instruction and trade confirm process may be different so that whilst the transaction cannot proceed to settlement if unconfirmed, instructions for settlement can be prepared and sent.

Once the two counterparties have confirmed trade details with each other, the next stage is to pass delivery/receipt instructions to the clearing organisation. The task of the clearing organisation is to:

- match delivery instructions with the corresponding receipt instruction (*see diagram below*), and to
- report the matching results back to the instructing counterparties.

Settlement Overview

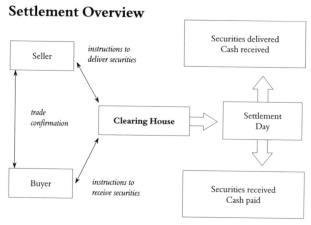

Figure 5.1   The role of the clearing organisation in securities confirmation

Those instructions which are matched are held by the settlement organisation in a pending file until the due settlement date arrives. No further action is required during this period. The processes of clearing and settlement needs to be explained as although there is a blurring of organisations onto multi-functional concerns, the actual process is quite distinct. Broadly, clearing is the process of recording, matching and confirming transactions, whilst settlement is the exchange of the asset for cash.

It is important to note here that with an increasing number of electronic trading systems being used in the markets, trade matching is becoming less of an issue as trades are effectively matched at the time of trade. However this doesn't mean that the dealer has performed the right trade, so internal trade matching to dealer's records/client orders is necessary. Problems arising from unmatched instructions must be resolved and correct instructions submitted to the clearing organisation for further matching. This stage must be completed in time to meet the clearing organisation's processing deadlines.

On settlement day, if there are sufficient assets, cash and securities, available for delivery, the trades will settle. The counterparties are advised of their securities and cash movements and, finally, securities ledgers and cash accounting records are updated to reflect these movements.

Definition: *Settlement is defined as the delivery of an asset in exchange for the equivalent in cash value.*

Problems of definition arise of "exchange" when the mechanics are looked at more closely. For example there is the risk of non-receipt of funds if settlement is made by cheque. The cheque takes time to clear and might subsequently be dishonoured by the payer. To reduce this risk, the cash element of settlement should be made in such a way that the cash is both *assured* (ie, guaranteed) and in *same day funds*.

Furthermore, settlement of securities and cash should take place at the same time and without the possibility of one party to the transaction countermanding the delivery or payment. Settlement should therefore be the *simultaneous and irrevocable* transfer of ownership of the securities in exchange for the agreed cash value, otherwise known as *Delivery Versus Payment* (DVP). In the markets, settlement periods range from T+0 to T+5. Most government bonds tend to settle on T+1 whilst corporate bonds generally settle on T+3. Equities tend to be longer T+3 and higher. Derivatives can be T+1 or periodic settlement amounts based on time and or events that trigger a payment/delivery.

So which organisations are involved in the clearing and settlement process and how does it impact in terms of different products?

Clearing Houses and Securities Depositories obviously are at the heart of the process and whilst there are similarities in the ways in which bonds, equities and derivatives settle, there are local variations to be aware of. Let us look at some bond settlement issues first.

International bonds, global bonds and convertible bonds are settled by for example two clearing houses, Euroclear and Clearstream. Not only can participants of one clearing house settle trades with another participant of the same clearing house, but also with participants of the other clearing house. This is known as settlement via the (electronic) bridge which exists between Euroclear and Clearstream.

Through their links to each other and to external depositories and CSDs, Euroclear and Clearstream are able to accept instructions to settle the following types of transactions:

Internal Settlements - these occur between two counterparties who are both participants of the same clearing house.

Bridge Settlements - these occur between two counterparties one of whom is a participant of Euroclear and the other a participant of Clearstream.

External Settlements - these occur between a local counterparty and a participant of Euroclear or Clearstream across a range of domestic securities.

Other types of services are offered by these organisations for instance Euroclear provide secured financing facilities to eligible participants for the purposes of covering securities settlements, pre-advising receipts of funds and, where appropriate, securities borrowing activities. The facilities are secured with cash and/or securities collateral.

Clearstream provide different types of financing including:

1. Unconfirmed Funds Facility
2. Technical Overdraft Facility
3. Tripartite Financing Agreement.

Details of Clearstream's facilities can be found at their website, see appendices.

The use of these facilities needs to be assessed from both a convenience and a cost point of view. As part of the overall process of asset management, the manager needs the ability to both ensure compliance with the settlement convention and the maximising of cost controls. Shortening settlement cycles will put further pressure on firms and managers to meet settlement deadlines and so arranging both funding lines and stock sources will become key functions in the operations team.

To help facilitate timely settlement of equity and bond transactions, both clearing houses operate borrowing and lending programs. In the UK, CREST offer a similar service. These facilities can be automatic so that for a firm short of stock for settlement will automatically be able to borrow securities and effect settlement on the due date. This kind of facility needs to be researched for its cost implications and also in terms of whether it is mandatory or an option. As we have seen, part of the asset management process is the ability to ensure availability of cash and securities on settlement date. We can explore this further.

The prime objective is to ensure that there is sufficient cash available to cover all purchases. Inability to pay for securities when presented by the seller for settlement, will result in a *failed settlement* and an interest claim from the settlement date up to the date on which the purchase finally does settle.

A secondary objective is to make effective use of any cash balances (whether uncommitted funds or funds expected or needed for trade activities) and in so doing enhance the returns and reduce costs. The level of interest received on credit balances and paid on overdrafts and credit facilities can be affected by the timing of the deposit of funds or use of the credit facilities. It is important for the manager to ascertain what, if any interest is paid on credit balances and charged on debit balances. These returns or charges add to the overall cost of the bargain and, over a year in a high volume operation if not monitored against alternatives, can be substantial.

Efficient management of this cash relies on accurate and timely information and communication between operations, treasury, clients and clearing houses. Cash positioning comes under an activity often referred to as cash management. The positioning of cash is part of the cash management process, which includes cash inflows and outflows from both transactions and also non-trading events such as:

Outflow	Inflow
• Call payments on partly paid bonds • Subscription monies for warrant exercise • Payments of uncommitted cash balances for money market purposes • Fees, charges etc.	• Interest receipts • Full/partial redemption proceeds • Receipts of cash to cover anticipated purchases

Table 5.2   An illustration of cash flow movements for the positioning of cash

Efficient cash management therefore seeks to anticipate future cash movements from a variety of sources in order to ensure that cash is in the right place at the right time, to reduce funding costs and to enhance returns on uncommitted cash balances.

Predicting future cash balances is straightforward when sales, purchases and other events take place as expected. This becomes more problematic when trades fail as it is not usually possible to know the settlement outcome until it has actually taken place. In addition, there will be separate instruction deadlines for transferring sufficient cash to meet the underlying obligation. The issue is further complicated by settlement of derivatives where there is no such situation as a settlement fail and cash must be paid to cover obligations by a set time or default procedures may result. As well as cash there is the issue of securities that need to be delivered and so securities positioning for sales and therefore deliveries is important. Again the issue of derivatives arises as settlement of securities for delivery against derivative transaction must take place at the time stipulated by the derivative exchange and clearing house. Any failure to meet this deadline can result in huge fines and or default.

So in addition to the cash funding issues for buyers, sellers must ensure that there are sufficient securities available for delivery. If a scenario arises whereby there are or there are likely to be insufficient securities available (through previous failed purchases, turnarounds, short selling, etc.), steps must be taken to record the reasons and to deal with this situation. This is covered by what is often known as Fails Control and we look at this later in the chapter of the book.

Regular reports are provided from clearing houses or custodian organisations listing all the current securities and cash balances and often will include warnings of any potential or actual restrictions to securities deliveries and cash payments.

We mentioned fails control earlier and clearly when a settlement fail occurs or is highly likely to occur, action is needed by the team. It is imperative that clear procedures are developed and understood to ensure that relevant action is undertaken and the action is reported internally and externally as appropriate.

However well the pre-settlement processing has gone, there will be settlement failures and these will not always be the fault of our firm, or indeed the immediate counterparty to us. For instance we see in the following list that a seller to us may be unable to fulfil that settlement. This is because securities to fulfil the settlement of this trade have not been received from a counterparty due to deliver them. There are many reasons for settlement failure, including:

Reason	Cause
There are insufficient bonds available for delivery	Selling participant may: • be unable to borrow • be unable to recall bonds out on loan • be awaiting receipt of bonds from purchase
There is insufficient cash	Buying counterparty may: • have cash funding or payment problems • be awaiting proceeds from a sale
Trade instructions are unmatched	• One or both counterparty(ies) has/have failed to input correct details • Both counterparties are in dispute • Operational error
Securities are unavailable for delivery	Clearing organisation has blocked deliveries in respect of a corporate event or action.

Table 5.3   Reasons and causes for settlement failure

A failed trade will result in one or more of the following situations:

*   One failed settlement might prevent other trades from settling either through lack of securities in sufficient quantity or insufficient cash
*   Funding costs and interest claims will occur
*   Resolving failure problems takes up valuable staff resources

- Organisations who repeatedly cause trades to fail will get a bad reputation in the market and may suffer action by the exchange or clearing house and on markets where the counterparty is known at the time of trade, a reluctance by firms to deal with the organisation
- The failure could be related to a derivative delivery requirement
- Regulatory capital implications.

As well as understanding why a settlement has failed, it is important to have procedures to resolve failed settlements. Depending on the circumstances, the choices are to wait until there are sufficient securities or cash available, or for the seller to try and borrow the securities. If these options are inappropriate, there are two formal courses of action available.

- *Seller is unable to deliver bonds.*
  The buyer has the right to issue a "buy-in" notice to the seller whereby the buyer purchases the bonds from another counterparty ("buy-in" agent) who has sufficient bonds to settle the trade. The original trade is then closed-out and the difference in cash amounts settled between the seller and buyer. This may be an option for the buyer or a mandatory action initiated by the market/clearing house and the rules will vary from market to market.

- *Buyer is unable to receive securities*
  The seller has the right to close the trade by means of a "sell-out". In this case, the seller sells the bonds to another counterparty ("sell-out" agent). The difference in transaction monies plus loss of interest on the sale proceeds is settled between the seller and buyer. Again this may be mandatory.

However, are there steps that can be taken to reduce the risk of a settlement fail.

In markets with high volumes, the turnover in a particular issue might exceed the total amount of the issue itself or exceed the amount of security "available" in the market. This can easily occur with bonds as they are often held to maturity by investors and not traded. This fact, allied to the pressure from derivative products like futures or options where large exposures have been built up and may go to delivery at a single date, can create real problem in the settlement chain. It might be appropriate for a market to settle trades on a net basis rather than a gross (ie, trade for trade) basis. Depending on volumes, the options are as follows:

- Trade for Trade
- Bilateral Netting
- Multilateral Netting
- Continuous Net Settlement
- Real Time Gross Settlement.

Netting is a process that reduces the risk of a default by creating a single settlement based on the netted credit and debit balances on long and short positions between counter-parties (Bilateral Netting). There are issues with netting not least of which is a legal one concerning enforceability of netting agreements, however the influential G30 recognised netting as a significant risk reducing tool and have encouraged changes to make its use more easy. In FX markets CLS Bank is looking to provide a clearing system that will settle transactions real time removing risk of default on one side of a deal.

WORK SESSION

Research netting and consider the advantages in terms of risk management and operational efficiencies. Also find out what "Herstatt Risk" refers to.

One way of quantifying the magnitude of settlement failures is to compare the actual percentage of transactions which settle on time (ie, on the original contracted settlement date) with a benchmark.

One particular benchmark covering settlement performance has been built by GSCS Benchmarks who state that the purpose of this benchmark is to:

> "...provide a means of comparing the settlement efficiency of different markets and track the evolution... over time. The benchmark incorporates the four components which combined together, reflect the overall cost to market participants of failed trades."

Source: GSCS Benchmarks

The funding costs associated with interest charges and lost opportunities to promptly re-invest cash balances can over time amount to a significant financial impact on a business if it is not monitored and dealt with. The direct market participants such as the dealers, brokers and market makers will also be obliged to consider the impact of failed settlements on the organisations requirements under regulation and risk capital. Any need to bring in further capital to cover this area obviously increases the cost to the organisations concerned.

With most types of securities there are corporate actions. A major operations function is dealing with corporate actions. Custody is a term that relates to a number of services that take place before or after settlement. Once settlement (or before settlement in the case of a trade where settlement is outstanding) has occurred, further settlement activity might occur as the result of a change to the security, for instance, a convertible bond or a benefit accruing to the holder of a security that is held, ie, interest. These types of changes are called corporate actions.

We know that a security has been settled and will be kept in safekeeping for as long as the investor or firm owns the security. A simple example of a corporate action is an interest payment due on a bond or money market instrument. It is imperative to not only know when such a payment is going to be made, but to also ensure that it is received and booked trough the accounts correctly.

The following table shows interest payment rules for a selection of bonds:

Security Type	Normal Rules
UK Government (Gilts)	Gilts go "ex" seven business days before the interest payment date. (An exception is the 3½% War Loan which goes "ex" ten business days before the payment day.)
International/Eurobonds (held by Euroclear and Clearstream)	Both Euroclear and Clearstream use a record date to establish which bond holders are entitled to receive the interest payment. The record date is usually the close of business, one day before the payment date of the interest. After the record date, settlements are processed ex-coupon.
German Bonds	The record date is the close of business, one day before the payment date of the interest.
Netherlands	The record date is the close of business, one day before the payment date of the interest.
Denmark	The record date is one month and one day before the payment date of the interest.
Japan • Samurai Bonds (Bearer) • Samurai Bonds (Reg'd) • Daimyo Bonds • Shogun Bonds (Bearer) • Shogun Bonds (Reg'd)	Record date prior to interest payment is: • 6 business days in Tokyo • 21 calendar days • 1 business day • 1 business day in Tokyo • 21 calendar days
Australian Global Bonds	The record date is 14 days before the payment date of the interest.

Table 5.4   Interest payment rules for bond securities

Remember that the terms of securities and their related corporate actions can be varied and it is crucial to keep information such as that shown above closely and constantly monitored. Once the correct beneficiary has been identified, all that remains is for the interest to be paid. In a manual process, the coupon will be detached from the bond certificate before being presented to the issuer's paying agent. The relevant amount of interest, as indicated on the coupon, is paid to the presenter of the coupon. In dematerialised/immobilised scenarios the coupon value is paid to the holder in the book-entry system.

Bond issuers usually make interest payments on either an annual or semi-annual basis, although there are bonds on which interest is paid quarterly. There are different interest conventions for different types of bonds as shown overleaf.

FIXED RATE BONDS

In the case of fixed rate bonds, where the amount of interest does not change throughout the life of the bond, the amount of interest and the payment date will be printed on the coupon.

FLOATING RATE NOTES (FRNS)

Interest rates on FRNs fluctuate with movements in the money markets. As the interest rates change, it is not possible to print the amounts on the coupons. For this reason, the FRN coupons will differ slightly from the fixed rate coupons.

Issuers advise bond holders of the new interest rate and next payment date by advertising the details in newspapers such as the *Financial Times* and informing the Clearing Houses, Euroclear, Clearstream etc, through their depository banks.

For holders of International/Eurobonds held by Euroclear and Clearstream's depositories, their cash accounts will be credited on the payment date with same-day value (the exception being Yankee Bonds, a dollar bond issued in the US by a non-resident, which pay with next-day value).

If, however, a trade, dealt "cum" (cumulative ie, including the coupon rather than "ex" without or excluding the coupon) does not settle until after the record date, the coupon is paid to the bondholder who held the bonds on Record Date, ie, the seller.

The systems automatically recognise that the rightful recipient of the coupon should have been the buyer and the result is that the seller's cash account is debited and the buyer's cash account is credited with the full coupon payment. In addition to any coupon entitlements, there is also the capital repayment by the issuer to the bond holder either on maturity, or in some cases earlier. A repayment of capital occurs when there is a partial or full return of the bonds to the issuer in exchange for cash. The terms of any repayments will be included in the original issue prospectus.

There are several instances were this might take place:

- Final Redemption
- Early Redemption (via an issuer's call option)
- Early Redemption (via a bondholder's put option)
- Partial Redemption (drawing).

Typically the depositories will present the bonds for repayment and debit the participants' securities accounts and credit the cash accounts with value on the repayment date. In order to allow sufficient time to surrender the bonds, the depositories will usually block the positions in order to prevent any further bond movements.

With convertible bonds, we have another type of consideration and therefore need to have suitable procedures in place. A bond holder is entitled to convert to another bond or equity as per the terms of the convertible bond, during a conversion period, usually at any time from 90 days after the bond was issued up to the final redemption date. However, any accrued interest is lost on conversion and the price of the bond must allow for the lost interest when calculating the conversion premium. The bondholder instructs the custodian to withdraw the bonds from custody (from the depository bank) and to deliver them to the conversion agent. The conversion agent will execute the conversion in accordance with the terms of the issue and local market practice.

The shares that have resulted from the conversion are subsequently delivered in accordance with the bondholder's original conversion instructions. There may be a delay before the shares are made available to the shareholder or custodian especially if they are in certificated form.

There are also bonds which are issued "cum-warrant". These warrants can be split away from the host bond and be exercised at the holder's option into a specified amount of shares at a pre-determined price and at a set time(s) in the future. This "purchase" or exercise requires the payment of cash to the issuer of the warrant.

The exercise price and the date or period during which the exercise might take place are given in the subscription terms of the warrant. An exercise may take place at a time pre-specified by the issuer. These are

- On an annual date; *or*
- During a pre-defined period; *or*
- At any time.

In terms of giving instructions to exercise their warrant, the holders do much the same as with conversions except that an additional amount of cash must be paid to the issuer in exchange for the underlying shares.

With other types of conversion, custodians will for instance convert the various types of *Depository Receipt* (American, Global, etc) into the underlying shares and will arrange delivery of these in accordance with the investor's instructions and local market practices.

It is important that adequate procedures are in place to ensure that reconciliation of securities and cash movements takes place.

There are many different situations when securities are received and delivered and cash is paid and received. These can happen together by transactions being settled on a delivery versus payment (DVP) basis or separately ie, conversion of bonds into equity, partially or in full.

For all transactions and settlement actions whether securities or cash related, market participants will keep accurate records of all movements and positions. This is known as reconciliation. Reconciliation is the front line and defence line for the protection of a business. Reconciling cash movements against transactions, positions and delivery are fundamental controls against rogue dealers, fraud etc.

Reconciliation can be described as the process by which cash and securities ledger positions are agreed to a third party's records with any differences or imbalances identified, investigated and resolved without delay. Operations managers must ensure the quality and robustness of the reconciliation processes are adequate and that the reconciliation staff understand the processes and how to act on and escalate any discrepancy effectively.

Cash, Bank, Nostro reconciliations are relatively straightforward to process insofar as the bank statement is compared to the ledger either manually or electronically and any unreconciled items recorded. These outstanding items must be monitored by operations managers and relevant action taken if they are not addressed promptly.

The following basic steps are applied:

1. Compare bank statement to ledger
2. Identify and record bank statement entries that cannot be identified
3. Identify and record ledger items for which there is no bank statement entry
4. Prepare reconciliation sheet or review electronic reconciliation
5. Identify and refer to operational sections for investigation and correction.

What makes manual cash reconciliations so problematic is the sheer quantity of items that pass over a client's account especially when the client uses several of the bank or brokers services. For the fund management company, payments and stock movements will go through the custodian for the fund often on instructions from the fund management operations team. Reconciliation of these instructions is imperative.

Reconciliation of securities at the depot and cash records are performed by comparing the investor's ledger records to those of the custodian or ICSD. The investors reconciliation is based on trade date. The custodian's records reflect the actual (settled) position. Not surprisingly there will be differences and these can include:

- trades pending settlement
- failed settlements
- corporate actions
- securities lending and borrowing positions
- bond positions blocked for whatever reason by the custodian.

These and any additional differences should be investigated, reported and action taken to resolve then immediately. The following flow could apply:

1. Compare custodian's balance to ledger via automated reconciliation or manually ticking-off items that match
2. Identify and record ledger items for which there are no corresponding custodian balances
3. Identify and record custodian items for which there are no ledger records
4. Prepare reconciliation and outstanding queries data and management reports
5. Ensure that outstanding items are investigated and resolved.

As part of the regulatory environment in most jurisdictions in the world, there are specific rules that deal protecting customers. In the UK, the *Financial Services Authority* (FSA):

- specify detailed record-keeping requirements requiring routine reporting and reconciliations with the records of customer investments held.

As one might expect, the comprehensive reporting services provided by the custodians in general and the ICSDs in particular include reports covering all the custody operations events. Examples of these types of reports follow:

- *Preliminary Advice/Information Reports*
  - FRN coupon fixing
  - Forthcoming redemptions
  - Forthcoming coupon payments
  - Conversion opportunity timings
  - Exercise opportunity timings.

- *Portfolio Position Reports*
  - List of securities held
  - Valuation of portfolio in currency of securities/base currency of investor.

Depending on the nature of the reports, the custodians will communicate by one or other of mail, telex, proprietary system or SWIFT messages. What kind operational issues and controls arise for the manager?

In the post trade environment, it is the role of the operations teams to ensure that, for example:

- The trades are verified
- Details are correctly uploaded into the relevant databases
- Dealers sign-off their agreement of position balances
- All trades are correctly processed
- Failed trades are identified and any discrepancies resolved
- Cash balances and securities positions are reconciled and outstanding items chased
- Derivatives margin is reconciled and covered.

As the majority of trades are settled on a "true" or "real" DVP basis, ie, simultaneous and irrevocable, the risk of one half of the trade settling and the other half failing is eliminated. This is an important control and therefore any trades settling free of payment need to be approved by managers. This extra attention must be paid to deliveries on a free of payment basis, especially if this is outside the normal market practice for that particular product. The following schedule illustrates some of the main issues and controls required to protect the organisation from risk exposure and potential financial loss:

Activity	Operational Issue	Controls
Trade Verification	• Trade date • Settlement Date • Price Tolerances • Approved Products • Settlement Instructions	Reference to market settlement conventions Pre-specified price limits Dealer authorities and limits Reference to counterparty/client standing instructions
New Products New Clients	• Details of clients and products must be correct and current • Unnoticed/incorrect information will have an adverse impact on any dealings • There are regulatory implications associated with clients	Full details of product should be obtained and checked before release into the database
Position Agreement (Dealer's "Blotter")	Trade dealt and dealing positions should agree with the dealer's own records	Daily reconciliation of blotter to settlement's records. Any discrepancies should be resolved by close of business
Trade Confirmation	Trade details must be in agreement with those of the counterparty (the confirmation, once agreed, becomes a legally binding contract).	There are various ways to generate and transmit confirmations. All outgoing confirmations should be ticked-off against the trade and incoming confirmations checked and discrepancies dealt with on trade date.
Trade Instructions	Clearing systems can only settle those trades which have been submitted by both counterparties and matched.	Unmatched trade reports should be reviewed and appropriate action taken before settlement date.
Cash Funding	There should be sufficient cash available to cover all requirements. This is a predictive activity which considers previous fails and future needs.	Cash predictions should be made daily in sufficient time to meet treasury/bank/clearing system deadlines.
Securities Balances	There should be sufficient balances "available for delivery", otherwise there will be failed settlements to deal with.	Use of securities borrowing will reduce the incidence of failed sales. (Uncommitted positions should be considered for lending purposes.)
Review Settlement Results	Settlement fails cause funding inefficiencies and further delivery problems. There will also be concerns of exposure to counterparty risk and regulatory requirements to increase financial resources i.e. extra capital)	Reports should be prepared by product type, counterparty and dealer for analysis. Failed trades should be chased and use of buy-ins & sell-outs where appropriate.

Product Lending and Borrowing Activities	Issues cover: a. loan/borrow initiation b. collateral receipt c. repricing outstanding loans and collateral d. income collection and corporate actions activities e. interaction with other operational units (dealers, settlements etc.)	Activities must be covered by a standard lending agreement and adequately margined collateral. Outstanding positions should be monitored and reported to associated departments.
Nostro Reconciliation	Key control ensuring that cash ledger positions agree to bank statements.	Unreconciled positions should be investigated and resolved. Reports should be prepared for review by management.
Depot Reconciliation	Key control ensuring that securities positions agree to depository statements allowing for settlement fails, securities loans and borrows and any other relevant activities.	Unreconciled positions should be investigated and resolved. Reports should be prepared for review by management.
Corporate Actions	Information on corporate actions should be obtained and verified in time to allow the client/dealer to make a decision within the issuer's deadlines. Failure to instruct on time exposes the organisation to financial loss.	Extra care is required through use of diary systems and constant verification of event processes and deadlines.
Income Collection	Income on registered securities will be paid to the beneficiary, income on bearer securities will be claimed from the issuer. The correct amount of income considers tax situations and trades dealt cum- and ex-dividend.	Reports will indicate which cash payments will need to be claimed from the market or paid direct. Any claims for income or WHT reclaims should be prepared and chased.

Table 5.5   Illustration of the issues which arise from operational activities and the suggested controls

Supporting these control activities will be the Internal Audit team.

Their role includes:

- Ensuring the adequacy of Management Information Systems
- Reconciliation control where there are differences in valuation methodologies or systems used by the Front Office and Operations Department
- Increasing the depth and frequency of audits where weaknesses and significant issues are brought to light or significant changes have been made to:

1. product lines
2. modelling methodologies
3. risk oversight processes
4. internal controls, *or*
5. the overall risk profile of the organisation

- Facilitating the development of adequate controls by being brought into the product development cycle at the earliest possible stage
- Evaluation of the independence and overall effectiveness of the organisation's Risk Management functions.

Now let us look at equities and equity derivatives and consider the clearing and settlement issues for these products. As we know, when an investor purchases an equity instrument he/she is buying partial ownership in the issuing company. An investor's amount of ownership in a company is determined by the number of shares owned by the investor in proportion to the total number of shares outstanding.

An equity instrument may offer the following "*rights*" to investors:

- The right to vote in company matters
- The right to have access to company books and records (accounting and record keeping)
- The pre-emptive right (or right of first refusal). This means that if the company issues new securities, the current holders may have the right to purchase additional shares to maintain their proportional ownership of the company. This offer to the original holder is generally given before the offer is made to the public
- The right to share in the company's profits through dividend payments.

The different classes of equity instruments each have different rights attached to them. If you recall there are:

- Ordinary Shares
- Preference Shares
- Redeemable shares
- Convertible Preference Shares
- "A" or Non-Voting shares
- Deferred shares.

In overseas markets there may be similar products but with different terminology. For example:

- USA - Common Stock/ Preferred Stock
- France - Action Ordinaire (Ordinary Share)
- Germany - Stamm-Aktie (Ordinary Share)
- Japan - Futsu Kabushiki (Ordinary Share)

Ordinary shares represent partial ownership in a corporation. Typically the shareholders will:

- have the right to vote in the election of the board of directors
- have the pre-emptive right to purchase any additional shares sold by the company
- receive a dividend, but only if the directors decide to issue a dividend.
- generally receive a declared dividend only after preferred shareholders have been paid.

In addition, if the company is liquidated, (un)secured creditors, bondholders, and preferred shareholders have a prior claim to the company's assets before the common shareholders.

Preference shares also represent ownership in a corporation. Characteristically shareholders will:

- generally have no voting rights
- generally receive dividends before the ordinary shareholders.

The dividend is frequently fixed as a percentage of the share's stated value. However, the dividend is not guaranteed. If the company does not post strong earnings, the directors can omit the preferred dividend.

A cumulative feature may be attached to a preference share, which states that all dividends in arrears must be paid to holders at some point in time prior to any dividends paid to common shareholders.

Participating preference shares may benefit from an increased level of dividends if the company does well. Redeemable preference shares have a fixed repayment date and may be entitled to more than their nominal capital amount (Face value).

Preference shareholders generally have priority over ordinary shareholders to the company's assets in the event of bankruptcy or liquidation.

In addition some issues have features such as:

- a "callable" feature which stipulates that the issuer may, at a time or times as is in the provisions of the issue, call an issue for redemption
- a feature making the shares "convertible" to common shares.

There some companies that issue shares with restricted or no voting rights. These shares are entitled to receive dividends and, in the event of a liquidation, they rank alongside the ordinary shareholders. Deferred shares usually do not qualify for a dividend until the company's profits have reached a pre-set level, or until a particular date. So we have the basic characteristics of equities and the manager will need to devise procedures to reflect those differences. We can take this further in terms of specific situations such as when shares are first issued.

We know that when a corporate entity offers its shares to the public for the first time, it is said to be going public. This "Offer for Sale" or Initial Public Offering (IPO) will be underwritten by investment banks or brokers. A prospectus containing information on the issuer, the terms of the issue, the management structure and any other important aspects of the issuer is prepared. The issue itself will either be placed amongst clients of the brokers (institutional investors) or advertised to the general public through the publication of mini-prospectuses and application forms in the financial press and elsewhere.

Any shares which are not bought by the public will be taken-up by the underwriters (underwriters agree to take up any shares not applied for) who will take the shares onto their own books or sell them on to their own clients. On the other hand, issues that are initially over-subscribed will be distributed on a scaled-down basis. One of the consequences of an over-subscription is that the share price will rise to a premium over the issue price. Transactions in shares are processed in much the same way as with debt instruments, ie, trade confirmation followed by instruction matching and final settlement. There are however some differences both in terms of methodology and performance.

As shares are becoming increasingly immobilised or dematerialised, this enables shares to be delivered by book entry rather than by physical transfer. Whilst this is helping to overcome problems with equity settlement it is a fact that equities currently have longer settlement periods compared to debt and derivative products.

As with debt market instruments, equities transactions will also be settled and held through third party organisations. In some markets, the clearing house will be independent from the depository or one and the same entity. Today many clearing houses and depositories deal with a cross-section of products including bonds, shares, warrants, convertible bonds and unit trust shares.

In the UK, CREST and the LCH have from February 2001 provided settlement of equities on T+3 and a Central Clearing Counterparty facility (EquityClear). This is a similar arrangement to that used for exchange traded derivatives and is also in use on Euronext, the combined Belgian, Dutch and French securities and derivatives markets through the clearing house Clearnet.

We know, from looking at bonds earlier in the chapter, that there are various types of corporate action. With equities there are various benefits that are distributed. A benefit distribution is a distribution made by a company to its shareholders in the form of cash, securities or a combination of both in cases where an entitlement is a fraction of a share. Distributions are usually made in proportion to the investor's holding as at the record date. The prime example would be a cash benefit such as a dividend, to shareholders on a regular basis. This would be typically on a semi-annual or quarterly basis. As the dividends are paid from profits, the amount of cash paid will change from payment to payment.

As the majority of equities are in registered form, it is theoretically straightforward for the issuing company to identify the beneficiaries. If the shares are in bearer form rather than registered securities, the issuer will require some form of proof before making a payment; this proof, as with bearer bonds, is in the form of a coupon which is detached from the share certificate.

A problem arises for a "cum-dividend" purchaser, whose name is not recorded on the company's share register in time to receive the dividend.

In order to establish correct entitlement, it is important to understand how some key dates come into play. These dates are:

- record date
- pay date
- ex-date (ex-dividend date).

The record date is the date upon which the issuer or the Registrar closes its books for the purpose of capturing the names of the legal owners to whom the distribution will be paid. All legal owners will participate in the distribution, whether or not they are the beneficial owners. In other words, the issuer will pay the "registered holder" even if the shares have been sold. As they will need to be re-registered in the new owners name, it follows that until such time as re-registration is performed, the seller is still the legal owner and therefore the initial recipient of any benefits. Clearly it is important that there are procedures in place to ensure that entitlements such as dividend benefits are claimed if the shares were not registered in time. As certificated securities are traded, the buyer (the new beneficial owner), or their fiduciary agent (broker, bank custodian), should submit the physical shares to the Registrar (or Transfer Agent), appointed by the issuing corporation to handle such transactions. The Registrar will cancel the old certificate(s) and issue new ones. The new beneficial owner (or its nominee) has now become the new legal owner.

With dematerialised and book entry settlement common in major markets, this process is all automated so therefore the operations manager must ensure that staff are clear on the procedures for both automated and residual certificated settlement processes. A list of owners will be supplied to the issuer's paying agent in order that they may disburse income payments to shareholders of record on the pay date. The pay date is the date on which the issuer or it's agent pays the distribution to the owners of record. The distribution of income payments to clients should take place on time ie, on pay date.

Note: The Paying Agent may be a Financial Institution or company treasurer who is named as the organisation or person responsible for disbursing payments to share/bond holders on behalf of the issuer.

The ex-dividend date (ex-date or xd) is the date upon which the security begins to trade without the declared benefit, for example in the *Financial Times* we will see *xd* after the share price. Investors who purchase securities "cum" of the entitlement are entitled to receive any benefits that the issuer decides to distribute. In most cases the trade, once settled, will be processed by the Registrar who then substitutes the seller's name with the buyer's. Although the settlement should occur before record date, it is quite possible for a re-registration on such a purchase to be late. In this case the seller would receive the benefit although they are not being entitled to receive it.

In order to bypass this situation, the local stock exchange will determine a date (known as an ex-dividend date) after which any purchaser will buy without entitlement to the particular benefit. Instead the seller retains the benefit. This ensures that there should, in the majority of cases, be no need to initiate a benefit claim. Once the pay date has passed, everything reverts to normal.

A *capital repayment* is a partial repayment of a company's issued capital. The company pays each shareholder a proportion of the value of the shares at the current market price. Whilst the number of shares issued remains the same, the nominal value of each share is reduced by the amount of the capital repayment per share. Other benefits may be in the form of shares rather than cash. An example would be a rights issue.

A *rights issue* is a further issue of shares offered by a company to its existing shareholders and in proportion to their existing shareholdings as at a record date.

Shareholders are offered the right to subscribe for new shares on or before a pre-determined date in a ratio to their holdings at a price below the current market price. The custodian's first task is to provide all the clients who have a shareholding with full details of the issue including dates and payment amounts.

We can flag here another key issue for managers to consider in respect of any corporate action and that is where and how is information on these benefits obtained? Typically the information can be provided by one or more of the following:

- company/issuers announcement via the press and or exchange
- information service suppliers ie, Reuters
- custodians
- specialist data providers

- internal databases ie, coupon payment dates, expected dividend announcements.

Time is an important issue as decisions need to be made as we can see from the following options open to a shareholder.

Returning to rights issues, with a rights issue there are several options available to the shareholder:

- the nil-paid rights can be traded for cash
- the rights can be accepted and paid for by making a cash payment (known as a call payment)
- the nil-paid rights can be allowed to lapse, ie, neither traded nor accepted
- sufficient rights can be sold and, with the proceeds, the remaining rights taken-up.

Unlike a rights issue - which requires the shareholders decision - a capitalisation or bonus issue is mandatory. A capitalisation is the free issue of shares to existing shareholders in proportion to the shareholders' balances as at record date. In this case, the client does not need to give any instructions; however they should be informed of the issue by the global custodian as the number of shares will change and so will the price of the shares. Initially the market value remains unaltered.

Scrip dividends are a method companies use to distribute profits in the form of shares instead of cash. The shareholder is offered the basic benefit of receiving cash or given the option to receive shares. Entitlement to scrip dividends is based on shareholdings on the register as at record date. The number of shares offered takes into account the amount of dividend payable and the underlying market price of the shares.

The custodian must also ensure that the client's instructions are obtained and passed on. Although the company will usually pay the cash dividend in the absence of any instructions to the contrary, it is important to check the terms of the issue in case the basic offer is for scrip. In most cases, it is possible to issue standing instructions for future scrip dividends.

Other kinds of corporate actions or events that the manager must take into account in the workflow include the following:

- A *stock situation* is any event that changes the nature or description of a company's securities. Stock situations are either optional, where the shareholder has a choice, or mandatory, where the shareholder is required to accept the company's decision for the change.

- A *take-over* for instance is a situation in which a bidding company wishes to obtain a controlling interest in a target company. It is optional for the investor to the extent that he can accept or decline the offer within the deadline specified by the bidder. If, in the terms of the offer, the bidder agrees to take over 100% of the company on condition that there is, say, a 75% acceptance level, then the remaining shares are compulsorily acquired, ie, the situation becomes non-optional for those shareholders who did not accept the offer.

- A *warrant subscription* is optional and gives the holders of warrants the right to 'exercise' the warrant in exchange for equity by making a subscription payment to the issuing company. If they are not exercised by the last possible date, the warrants expire worthless.

- *Pari passu lines of a security* can cause many problems for the global custodian and investor alike. A company might issue securities which are identical to existing securities already in circulation except that, for a pre-determined period of time, the new securities do not qualify for a particular dividend or are subject to some other type of restriction. Once this period is over, the two lines of securities are merged and become *Pari Passu*; they rank equal in all respects. Until the two lines of securities become *Pari Passu*, they are given separate security codes and in addition will trade at different prices. Both global custodian and investor must be aware of these differences and reflect the holdings accurately in the safekeeping records.

- An investor of a company which goes into *liquidation* will be in the situation where the security is not only worthless but also un-negotiable. The security will be suspended in the relevant stock exchange(s) until such time as the liquidator is able to repay amounts due to the various classes of creditor. Once there is no more cash that can be retrieved for the creditors, the company is wound-up and the certificates cancelled. This process can take years to resolve and the global custodian must ensure that any information is passed to the client and that all expected liquidation payments are collected and paid to the client.

- *Proxy voting* has been defined by the as "the exercise of the voting right(s) of an investor in shares, bonds and similar instruments through a third party, based on a legally valid authorisation and in conformity with the investor's instructions." Depending on the country in which the 'proxy' is being exercised, the 'third party', can be:
  - a bank, or
  - a person designated by the company, or
  - another shareholder.

  Proxy voting generally takes place at shareholders' meetings of companies (Annual General Meetings and Extraordinary General Meetings) for the purpose of approving or rejecting certain pre-advised resolutions. Proxy voting can be subject to more or less stringent restrictions depending on national legislation and company by-laws. In each case, therefore, the legal aspects must be carefully examined.

- With *equity derivatives* and in particular stock options, the impact of corporate actions can be significant. With a rights issue for instance the strike/exercise price may be changed so too may the number of shares per contract. Developing procedures for information about corporate actions in underlying assets to be simultaneously and automatically passed to the operations team dealing with the derivatives products is vital.

Allied to this is the need to have operations staff trained to adequate competency in both derivatives and securities, and a successful manager will ensure that this happens.

What about the issues for managers in say a global custodian? Here there is the problem of collating sufficient information to allow the client to make a decision where appropriate and ensuring that the results of the corporate action or event are correctly received, recorded and accounted for.

Operational issues and controls for equities are generally similar to those required for debt securities. In terms of trade capture from the dealing or fund management desks, counterparty trade confirmation, trade instruction/matching within a third party clearing environment and final settlement, there should be no differences.

The areas where there will be differences include the following:

- poorer settlement performance, especially where certificated settlement is concerned and in emerging markets
- greater variety and complexity of corporate actions types
- issues associated with registered securities:
  - use of nominee names
  - street names
  - pooled and segregated holdings
  - timing issues for share re-registration
- less sophisticated or developed securities depository systems in some jurisdictions
- greater use of physical delivery and custody systems.

As we saw earlier in the chapter, there are times when settlement of securities might fail. One possible way of avoiding that situation is for a seller to borrow stock to effect the settlement on time. Stock lending and borrowing facilities are therefore important for different types of organisation, but equally they require very clearly defined procedures and careful monitoring of exposures.

Securities lending is the lending of equities and bonds by or on behalf of an investor to counterparties who are authorised to borrow securities in return for a fee.

Securities lending provides liquidity to the market by utilising securities that otherwise would be "side-lined" by being held in safekeeping.

The Group of 30 (G30), an industry body, recognised the importance of securities lending in their Recommendation No. 8 published in the late 1980s, which stated that:

> "Securities lending and borrowing should be encouraged as a method of expediting the settlement of securities transactions. Existing regulatory and taxation barriers that inhibit the practice of lending and borrowing securities should be removed."

Securities lending and borrowing is now widely accepted and permitted. Legal title to the securities passes from the lender to the borrower, but the beneficial ownership is retained by the lender. This means that the lender continues to receive income and retains the right to sell the securities in the stock market. The lender, however, does lose the right to vote. Income will not be paid direct to the lender as his name will have been removed from the company's register; instead the income is claimed from and paid by the borrower.

Market participants need to borrow securities for a variety of reasons, including:

- to cover short positions (where participants sell securities which they do not hold)
- to support derivatives activities (where participants may be subjected to an options exercise)
- to cover settlement fails (where participants do not have sufficient securities to settle a delivery).

Market participants are happy to lend securities to earn fee income. This has two benefits:

- Fee income enhances the investment performance of the securities portfolio.
- As securities lending decreases the size of the portfolio, there is a corresponding reduction in safekeeping charges.

Global custodians take advantage of securities lending and borrowing by acting as intermediaries in the process. The global custodians benefit by:

- Retaining a share of the fee income whilst running a discretionary lending programme for their client, and/or
- Charging a transaction fee for every movement across their client's securities account where the custodian is unaware of the reasons for the securities movements.

As a global custodian holds sizeable quantities of any particular issue, it is able to play an important role by providing liquidity to the market. Furthermore, lenders and borrowers benefit from increased operational reliability and reduced risk by using the global custodian's services such as:

- Clearance
- Payment
- Settlement

- Collateral Pledging
- Valuation (mark-to-market).

The chapter on custody explores the role and services in greater detail.

There is risk in lending stock. The lender is primarily concerned with the safe return of his securities by the borrower and that there are adequate means of recompense in the event that the securities are not returned.

There are four situations each of which could place the lender at a disadvantage:

1. The most serious situation is where a *borrower defaults* with no chance of the lender retrieving the securities
2. Timing differences between delivery of the loaned securities and the corresponding receipt of sufficient collateral
3. The late/delayed return of securities due to settlement and securities liquidity problems experienced by the borrower
4. Settlement inefficiencies or a systemic collapse within the local market itself.

Various countermeasures are taken in order to reduce the risk associated with each of the above situations. We can start by considering a default by a borrower.

Securities are delivered by the lender on a "free of payment" basis to the borrower. For his part, the borrower covers the loan by delivering collateral to the lender.

Clearly it is of utmost importance that the collateral should be of such quality and quantity that it must be readily exchangeable into cash in the event that the borrower defaults. With this type of liquid collateral the lender is able to replace the missing securities. So the manager needs to be aware of the implications of using cash and non-cash collateral in lending and borrowing situations. What is efficient, what is the risk policy as this determines what is accepted and also what is market practice in different jurisdictions. We look at some of these issues in more detail over the next pages.

As far as collateral quantity requirement is concerned, the borrower must obviously deliver collateral with a market value which exceeds the market value of the loaned securities (the outstanding loans) by a pre-determined margin.

This margin allows for any variation in the value of the outstanding loans. The securities out on loan are "marked-to-market" (priced at the current market value) at least daily using the previous business day's closing prices and sometimes intra-day in fast moving markets. Any resulting shortfall in the amount of collateral is made good by the borrower. Conversely, any excess collateral is returned to the borrower. Managing this process needs effective records, exposure assessments, collateral valuations and effective procedures calling for increased collateral. When a volatile market develops and we have day light exposure there is a real risk to the business.

Daylight exposure is the intra-day settlement risk that loan securities may be delivered before the collateral is received. If the borrower should then default during the intervening period, the lender would be unsecured. The reverse is also true for a loan return.

The following example illustrates the problem:

A lender who delivers securities to the borrower at 10:00 but does not receive the collateral until 15:00 has a daylight exposure of five hours.

There is a particular problem when the parties to a loan transaction and the domicile of the securities are all in different time zones.

eg,   Lender in London
       Borrower in New York
       Securities in Tokyo

Loan transaction for value Wednesday; securities delivered on Wednesday (Tokyo time zone).

Collateral due for delivery value Wednesday: collateral delivered Wednesday (New York time zone).

In the lender's time zone, there is an exposure of at least fourteen hours, ie, from the time the securities are delivered (before close of business in Tokyo) to the receipt of collateral (after start of business in New York).

We have established that delays in settlement can be caused by the usual settlement failure types:

- Insufficient securities to satisfy the total delivery
- Lender or borrower gives late or incorrect delivery/ receipt instructions.

For a market maker with a net "short" trading position these delays will have an impact on the settlement process unless there is a reliable source of stock lending..

Investors will always want to invest in countries where there are opportunities for capital gain and income growth and with scant attention to the efficient operation of the settlements systems. Emerging markets are a prime example of this. Securities lending does however depend on the ability to deliver securities without delays and complications. For this reason, securities lending is primarily undertaken in the established markets with reliable and robust settlement processes. Any stock lending and borrowing in emerging markets needs careful consideration by the operations manager. The ability to mitigate some of the risk through the use of collateral may not be sufficient and any direct stock lending arrangement may also be concerned with credit rating of the borrower. With discretionary lending programs run by for instance custodians, the default risk is theirs. To ensure that collateral is of the acceptable quality and liquidity the following types of collateral would be generally acceptable.

Cash where the lender places the cash out into the money markets and agrees to pay interest (a rebate) to the borrower at a rate lower than the market rate. The difference in rates reflects the lending fee payable to the lender.

Advantages of accepting cash as collateral:

- Acceptance of cash collateral allows the securities to move on a DVP basis and thus eliminates the risk that the securities delivery and collateral receipt do not occur simultaneously
- Cash is regarded as the safest form of collateral in domestic markets including the USA where it is used in the majority of cases.

Disadvantages of accepting cash as collateral:

- Operational issues – many institutional lenders are not prepared or able to undertake the extra administrative burden of reinvesting the cash
- The tax and regulatory situations in such countries as UK and Germany make the use of cash impractical
- There are the added problems of foreign currencies which require one or two day's notice prior to placing funds
- There is an exposure to adverse exchange rates when using foreign currencies.

Collateral in the form of other securities can be acceptable in certain circumstances. The market value of the collateral must also be margined and easily realisable into cash in the event of borrower default. Commonly acceptable types of securities used as collateral are:

- A *Certificate of Deposit* (CD) and *Treasury bills*. CDs are certificates which give ownership of a deposit at a bank and for both Treasury Bills and CDs there is an established market.

The advantages of using CDs as collateral are:

- Considered to be of high quality and "near-cash" they are guaranteed by the banks on which they are drawn. The lender is able to specify the credit-worthiness of the banks by only accepting paper with a rating of, say, "A" or better
- CDs are in bearer form and therefore straightforward to sell should the need arise
- Movements of CDs in the UK take place almost exclusively by book-entry within the Central Moneymarkets Office operated by the Bank of England through CREST.

The disadvantages of CDs as collateral are:

- The nominal amount of CDs tends to be in shapes or size of £1,000,000 or $1,000,000 and this makes it difficult to ensure that the margined collateral value matches the value of outstanding loans

- CDs have a limited lifespan and borrowers must ensure that CDs are substituted as old CDs mature.

Other forms of high-quality securities are sovereign and government bonds (UK Gilts, US Treasury Bonds, German Bunds and French OATs) which also benefit from high credit ratings and ease of sale.

Equities are used but the issuer creditworthiness and the high-risk nature of the security type itself are not generally acceptable to lenders. In addition, long settlement periods can delay the time from borrower default to receipt of the collateral sale proceeds.

Another popular method of providing collateral cover is a letter of credit issued by a bank. But their use is under threat as the cost of a Letter of Credit is making borrowing against them unprofitable.

Advantages of taking Letters of Credit as collateral:

- Lender does not need to reinvest or revalue the Letter of Credit.
- Daylight exposure (see below) is eliminated if receipt of a Letter of Credit is pre-advised to the lender before the securities are released to the borrower.
- Face amount of Letter of Credit is more than adequate to cover the margined value of the outstanding loans and this results in less collateral movement to maintain the margin levels.

Disadvantages of taking as collateral are:

- Credit risk of bank that issued the Letter of Credit.
- (For the borrower) the high cost of obtaining a Letter of Credit from the bank.

Any activity in lending and borrowing needs to be covered by an agreement, in this case a Stock Lending Agreement (SLA). In order to protect the interests of the lending parties, the borrowing parties and the intermediaries, agreement forms are drawn up to clearly define the rights, duties and liabilities of those concerned.

An agreement will contain references to, *inter alia*, the following topics:

Agreement Topic	Comments
Interpretation	Definitions of the terms used in the agreement.
Rights & Title	Includes reference to the protection of lender's entitlements.
Collateral	Loans should be secured with collateral.
Equivalent Securities	Securities and collateral should be returned in an equivalent form to the original deliveries.
Lenders' and Borrower's Warranties	Statement that both parties are permitted to undertake the lending/borrowing activities.
Default	Remedies available in the event that one or other party defaults on its obligations.
Arbitration & Jurisdiction	How and where disputes will be submitted for resolution and under which governing law.

Table 5.6   Clarification of the terms contained in stock lending agreements

The extent to which the global custodian is involved in stock lending and borrowing activity of an organisation depends on the type of service offered. Direct lending will suit the bigger investors who are able to offer portfolios with large and varied holdings. They are therefore able to earn higher fees by going direct to the market. Large life funds hold significant amounts of securities and would be "natural" lenders, however they must abide by the trust deeds and other conditions so will not always be involved in lending.

The key points are:

•   Investor negotiates loan agreements and recalls/returns with the intermediaries or borrowers
•   Investor controls the movement of collateral and ensures that margins are maintained
•   The investor assumes the counterparty risk of the intermediary
•   The global custodian delivers and receives securities on a "free of payment" basis on instructions taken from the investor.

The risks for the investor are that they assume all risks associated with stock lending including:

Intra-Day Exposure

Investor must ensure that securities are not released until adequate margined securities are under his control (directly in-house or indirectly through a global custodian or settlement agent).

Settlement Risk

Investor must ensure that deliveries of securities for loans are made on time.

Deliveries of securities "free of payment" demand a higher level of authorisation and control than deliveries made on a DVP basis.

Investor must be able to identify in sufficient situations where securities on loan are required to settle a sale transaction and to initiate timely recalls.

Market Risk

Collateral should be revalued more frequently in volatile markets.

Legal Risk

Investor is responsible for arranging and monitoring the legal stock-lending agreements.

The rewards are:

Fee Income

The investor receives the full amount of the fees.

Exposure

Investor is free to choose the intermediaries and not be part of a direct queuing system (*see below*).

Non-discretionary lending differs from direct lending insofar as the global custodian takes a more involved role in the process.

The key points are:

- The custodian seeks approval from the client for each loan request.
- The custodian receives collateral from the borrowers and ensures that the margins are adequate
- A fee is charged by the custodian for this service
- The client assumes the risk of the borrowers.

The extra advantage for the client is:

- The custodian ensures that the collateral is matched to the movement of securities
- The custodian is better placed to initiate timely loan recalls to cover the client's sales.

The disadvantage is:

- That the client's relationship with the intermediaries might suffer now that they approach the custodian for loan requests and returns.

Discretionary programmes tend to suit the small/medium-sized lenders whose individual holdings are not always large and varied enough to attract borrowers.

The stock lending is delegated entirely to the custodian in the following key ways:

- The custodian actively seeks to place securities out on loan with the intermediaries
- The custodian takes collateral and monitors the margins
- A portion of the risk of the borrower is transferred from the client to the custodian
- Depending on the level of risk assumed by the custodian, anything from 50-60% of the fee income is retained by the custodian.

The advantages for the investor are:

- The service is totally linked into the custodian's settlement systems thus ensuring that the risk of settlement failure through late recalls is almost eliminated
- The investor benefits from being a part of substantially larger holdings which may be more attractive to potential borrowers.

The disadvantages for the investor are:

- Depending on the method of loan allocation adopted by the custodian (*see below*) the investor's assets may not be fully utilised
- The investor receives only a portion of the fee income. However, this will be offset by reductions in transaction charges and safekeeping fees.

There is an issue which effects the ability of an investor to participate in securities lending on an equitable basis. This presents the global custodian with the problem of ensuring that loans, and fee income, are allocated fairly. To cope with this, the global custodians use sophisticated algorithms to allocate loans and fee accruals fairly. As stated earlier the lender loses legal ownership and the voting rights associated with the securities but retains the benefits of ownership. It is important to appreciate that the lender is treated as if he had not lent the securities; any shortfalls are made good by the borrower who, as temporary legal owner of the securities, will receive the benefits in the first instance. It is the responsibility of the intermediary or global custodian to ensure that the lender is not disadvantaged through securities lending activities.

This part focuses on the expectations of the securities lender and the actions which they must take in order to satisfy the lender's requirements. Therefore the manager must ensure that the impact of corporate actions on any stock lending or borrowing situation is identified and dealt with. Any inadequate procedures or competency in the operations team will lead to potential significant financial losses and loss of reputation.

We can recap on why companies create corporate actions, for instance:

Rights Issues
Raise cash in order to:
- finance acquisitions
- expand business
- reduce borrowings
- stay afloat.

Convertibles
Lower interest payments.

Warrants
Future cash inflow at no cost.

Capitalisation issues
Convert reserves into share capital.
Increase marketability by reducing price.

Repayment of share capital
Return surplus cash to shareholders.

We also know that the main types of corporate action fall into two key categories; those which are *optional* in nature and those which are *mandatory*. How does this impact in terms of lenders and borrowers? Lenders retain the right to participate in all dividends, interest payments and other benefits on securities that are on loan. The one exception is that the lenders loses the right to vote. It is therefore essential that lenders are able to focus on two areas by having certainty in the knowledge that incoming corporate action information is sufficient to ensure that they can make an informed decision and assurances that all decisions are dealt with in accordance with their instructions.

If securities are on loan over the record date, the issuing company will pay the dividend to the party at the end of the borrowing chain. The lender will therefore be paid an amount of cash in lieu of the actual dividend. In other words, the borrower manufactures a dividend payment in order to make the lender whole. The rules regarding overseas securities require manufactured dividends to be paid under a deduction of the *Withholding Tax* (WHT) applicable to the country of issue of the securities.

The lending intermediary's prime role is to ensure that the lender is "made whole" and this can be achieved in the following ways by:

- gathering information from numerous sources
- comparing information from one source with another to ensure consistency
- rearranging the information (including any translations) into a form from which the lender can make a decision
- ensuring that all expected instructions are received from the lenders
- giving accurate and timely instructions to the correct destination
- informing the lender of the corporate action results.

The need for the intermediaries to receive the lender's instructions in advance of the issuing company's own deadlines can cause problems with the lender. The lender might wish to delay a decision until the last possible moment; sometimes past the intermediary's deadline. Nevertheless the intermediary should, in this situation, attempt to comply with the instructions on a "best efforts" basis.

As we have already noted, information on impending events is obtained from a variety of sources, for example the issuing companies, central securities depositories, exchanges, the press and information vendors. The way in which the investor receives information depends very much on the nature of the event itself and the manner in which the investor chooses to hold the securities in safekeeping. We also know that all corporate actions have deadlines, especially those which require a decision (the optional events). Unfortunately, differing worldwide standards do not make the task of monitoring corporate actions any easier. For this reason, it is important for the intermediaries and/or their agents to ensure that the information received is accurate and that any instructions are given in the form and within the deadlines specified by the company. Failure to settle situations such as market purchases and sales on time will result in delays and inconvenience. There might be occasions when penalty interest is payable and both counterparties will be exposed to an element of risk whilst the trade remains unsettled. Remember also that the obligation to settle the trades remains until such time as the delivery of securities (together with the underlying cash payment) takes place. Remember also that with an optional corporate action, failure to give and act upon accurate and timely instructions will usually result in a loss of entitlement to the benefit. The defaulting party will have to purchase securities (if securities were to be the benefit) in the market and pay the extra costs.

Let's consider some of the actions that are needed.

Voting Rights

Lenders who wish to exercise their right to vote must arrange for the loans to be recalled in sufficient time to comply with local voting rules. These rules might call for the re-registration of the securities into the lender's (or their appointed nominee's) name or might necessitate the blocking of the shares until the Annual (or Extraordinary) General Meeting has taken place.

Sufficient time should be allowed for this to happen.

Corporate Actions

It is the responsibility of the borrower to ensure that the lender is made whole with respect to corporate actions. The borrower can either unwind the loan returning the securities to the lender or can take up any entitlements on behalf of the lender making any extra cash payments as and when required.

Implications for Collateral

There are two points to note with respect to collateral. The amount of collateral pledged may have to increase or decrease in order to maintain the required (margined) levels of cover. This applies equally to collateral that is taken in the form of cash or other securities (whether in the same currency or different currencies). If other securities are used, there will come a time when corporate actions will affect the collateral itself. In this case, the collateral can either be substituted or treated in much the same way as the loaned securities.

So clearing and settlement is varied and the challenge for the operations manager is to deal with the process flows. In the initial phases it is the trade confirmation process, settlement instructions and the management of the cash and securities positions prior to and over the settlement date. Additionally there will need to be in place adequate procedures and controls to ensure that issues like settlement fails, corporate actions, stock lending and borrowing and collateral are efficiently and safely handled. Some of the key areas to focus on will be information source and records ie, positions, actions etc, terms of lending agreements, recording and valuing of collateral and loaned securities and taking necessary action to adjust the level of collateral and or rebate and the way in which the decisions on optional corporate actions are received and instructions passed within the time constraints that exist.

Operations teams are obviously structured differently in organisations but the following two diagrams give a generic overview of the structures for (a) derivatives and (b) securities business.

Figure 5.7.1 An example of the structure of an operations team in a derivatives business

Figure 5.7.2 An example of the structure of an operations team in a securities business

To help this process we can look at completing a work session.

WORK SESSION

Think about the process flow from trade to settlement for a product and then consider the controls needed for post trade situations like different corporate actions and identify the likely problems. Look also at the ISSA Recommendations and consider how these have or will impact and what effect the problems you have identified will have in terms of operational risk.

The process of clearing and settlement does as we have seen in this chapter involve custodians in various ways and so in the next chapter we look more closely at the role of the custodian.

6

CUSTODY

We have already looked at how the role of custodians is important so we need to understand more about what they do and how that affects the operations teams within the custody provider and the organisations taking the custody services.

With access to sophisticated computer systems and a worldwide network of subcustodians, global custodians are in a position to deliver a variety of services to their clients. These services are often referred to by custodians as either core services or value-added services.

The range of services includes:

- the safekeeping of securities
- the maintenance of multi-currency securities and funds accounts
- the settlement of securities trades in domestic and foreign markets, free of or against payment
- the collection of dividends, interest and principal due for redemption on due date
- the exercising or selling of subscription rights and attending to other corporate actions as well as pending fails
- the reporting of transactions completed and the periodical delivery of hardcopy statements of account
- contractual or actual settlement date accounting

- contractual or actual income collection
- terminal or computer-to-computer links to pass on instructions and retrieve client information from the custodian's database
- customised multi-currency reporting and performance information
- securities borrowing and lending
- assistance with withholding tax claims
- handling/settlement of derivatives
- briefings on specific countries, in particular on emerging markets
- cash projection and cash management
- ensuring that physical certificates and associated documentation are in good order.

From a global custodian's perspective, core services are those which are so standardised that there is not a great deal of scope for any particular global custodian to differentiate its service from that of another global custodian. Any fundamental changes and improvements will affect the industry as a whole.

Value-added services, on the other hand, provide the global custodians with the opportunity to offer a markedly better service to their clients, and in so doing, enhance the global custodians' standing within the marketplace and improve their fee-earning capabilities.

Settlement is the final transfer of cash from the purchaser to the seller in exchange for the delivery of the securities to the purchaser.

Settlement conventions vary widely from country to country and especially in the following areas:

- *Physical delivery vs book entry transfer of securities.* Prior to the introduction of CREST in the UK, an investor had to physically lodge the share certificate together with relevant transfer documentation with a London Stock Exchange processing office prior to settlement.

  International/Eurobonds, held in electronic book entry form by Euroclear and Clearstream, are settled by *Book Entry Transfer* (BET). The securities accounts of the seller and the buyer are credited and debited respectively.

Over 10% of securities markets are still paper-based.

- *Rolling settlement vs fixed settlement dates.* In the majority of worldwide securities markets, trades settle on a rolling basis, ie, a fixed number of days after trade date in line with G30's Recommendation No.7, which recommended that settlement conventions should be changed from settlement of trades in a period, eg, in the UK equity trades transacted in a ten day account period all settled on a single date, to rolling settlement.

- *The length of elapsed time from trade execution to trade settlement.* In the United States, the settlement of equities and corporate bonds occurs within three business days from trade date (T+3). This was changed in June 1995 from the old T+5 convention.

G30 recommended that settlement of all types of securities should take place on a T+3 basis throughout the world. In theory, all securities transactions should settle on time and in accordance with local market conventions. This allows investors to make efficient use of their money, whether for funding a purchase or placing/reinvesting sale proceeds.

In reality, the ability to settle securities transactions on time varies from country to country and within security types.

We need to consider why trades fail and how this impacts on the custody services.

Examples are:

- Late/incorrect settlement instructions from a counterparty to the custodian or clearing agent
- Seller has insufficient quantity of securities to deliver either as a result of a failed purchase or, for example, a market maker's business decision to go short (ie, to sell securities that he does not have)
- Purchaser has insufficient funds to pay
- Certificated securities are not yet available from the registrar from a recent purchase to cover a sale: the registration process can take up to several months to complete.

Whilst there are individual market mechanisms, such as buy-ins, to help resolve these failures, the result is that securities administration becomes inefficient, exposure to risk increases and costs rise. Buy-ins permit the purchaser to achieve timely settlement by purchasing the securities from another agent. The securities are delivered and the extra costs passed on to the original seller. In some Far Eastern markets the buy-in process is automatically generated by the market together with financial penalties and, in some circumstances, suspension of the offending broker's trading licence.

In terms of settlement accounting, global custodians would credit sale proceeds and debit purchase costs on whatever date the trade actually settled. This is known as *Actual Settlement Date Accounting* (ASDA). The application of ASDA works in favour of purchasers as they will have the use of their funds for an extra few days and perhaps have the opportunity either to earn interest or place the funds on deposit for that period.

However, ASDA is a disadvantage to sellers who will be unable to use the funds until received. This can cause a knock on problem where the expected funds were committed for other purposes on the original settlement date. Overall, ASDA, in poorly performing markets, handicaps the investor by making it difficult to manage cash flow requirements and cash positions effectively.

The global custodians have approached this problem by making a commitment to the investor that funds will be debited or credited for good value (in this case on the original settlement date). This is *Contractual Settlement Date Accounting* (CSDA). It enables the investor to operate in the certain knowledge that the cash accounts will reflect the expected entries and balances.

However in one or more of the following circumstances the global custodian will protect himself from risk of non-performance of the trade by insisting on variations in its contractual commitments to the investor:

- CSDA is unlikely to be offered in those countries which the global custodians consider to have a substandard settlement infrastructure.
- Investors' settlement instructions which have missed a deadline will be considered received the following day by some global custodians. In other words, either the CSDA value will be applied on a later date or ASDA will be applied

- The global custodian retains the right to reverse cash entries in the event that trades remain unsettled after a particular length of time
- CSDA on a sale will not be provided if there are insufficient securities to satisfy the delivery.

Whichever accounting practice is used, it is in the global custodian's interests (and the investor's where ASDA is used) to apply pressure on the local stock markets and authorities to improve the settlement environment.

The objective is to pass an accurate and timely instruction from the investor to the Central Securities Depository or clearing agent based in the country of the security via the global custodian and subcustodian network.

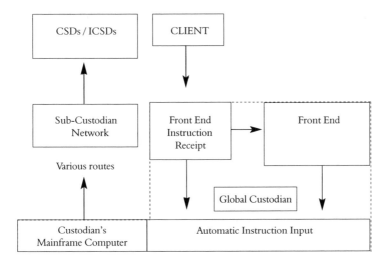

Figure 6.1   Example of Information Flows from client through to the CSDs via Global Custodian & Subcustodians
Source: the dsc.portfolio

There are numerous ways in which the investor is able to send a settlements instruction to the global custodian:

MANUAL/VERBAL INSTRUCTIONS

- Telephone instruction (with call back from the custodian to the investor) supported by a mailed confirmation from the investor
- Faxed instruction supported by a mailed confirmation from the investor
- Written instruction duly authorised by one or more officers of the investor
- Tested telex instructions in which the message is preceded by a series of digits uniquely identifying the instruction initiator to the receiving custodian and confirms to the custodian that the instruction may be acted upon. Usually, investors have the preparation of telexes automated within their systems.

These methods are in many ways inefficient and are not to be encouraged for the following reasons:

- Even though a telephoned instruction is called back correctly, there is no guarantee that the initiator of the instruction had the authority to issue the instruction
- Control is difficult to maintain in the absence of an effective and robust audit trail of the instructions
- It is not possible to authenticate with absolute certainty the location from which a faxed instruction was sent
- Written instructions can easily be delayed, mix-directed, or lost and the investor has no means of knowing if the instruction has been received until it is possibly too late to issue a replacement instruction.

All the above methods are to a greater or less extent time consuming and open to error and misuse.

ELECTRONIC INSTRUCTIONS

The investor enters instruction details into the global custodian's proprietary software installed in the investor's personal computers (PCs). The software converts the instructions into electronic data files which are then transmitted via a modem/telephone link to the global custodian's computer system.

Electronic transmission of instructions is preferable to manual methods for a variety of reasons:

- The software applications and the hardware in which it resides can be protected by both physical and electronic methods such as siting the PCs in a secure environment in the office and only allowing access to those staff who have authorised system identification numbers and user passwords
- The preparation of electronic instructions is faster and more accurate
- More effective controls can be established with full audit trails generated by the software
- Data files can be retained by using the archiving capabilities of the software thus dispensing with the need to retain large quantities of paper files.

There are three main methods by which the global custodian is able to communicate with the subcustodian. Which method is used depends to an extent on whether the subcustodian is a branch of the global custodian or a third party:

- If there is an own-branch relationship and both global custodian and subcustodian share the same systems technology, then trade instructions are transmitted through this medium.
- If the subcustodian is a third party or an own branch without a common technology, then instructions will be translated into a suitable message format and transmitted electronically through a communication network known as SWIFT.
- Tested telex.

The methods by which subcustodians communicate with the settlement agents and CSDs are dependent on local market practices. There are a number of issues which affect the ability of an investor to achieve timely settlement of overseas securities trades. Following the initiatives by G30, ISSA and other industry participants, global settlement practices are improving and timescales shrinking. There is a danger that if the lines of communication between investor and global custodian, global custodian and subcustodian and subcustodian and local market fail to meet the new settlement standards then settlement performance will be compromised.

With the final objective of a global convention of T+3 and then a reduction to a T+1 for equity settlement period, there is the problem of initiating a settlement instruction early enough to allow the global custodian to pass on the instruction to the sub-custodian and from there to the local market. The global custodian receives the investor's instruction and ensures that it is valid before passing it on to the subcus-todian. If this involves transferring the information from one system to another by a process of rekeying the data, then the risk of error and delay is high. Consequently, there is little time to correct any errors before settlement due date.

The solution is based on the ability of the investor to prepare and transmit a data file of information (ie, the settlement instructions) to the local market without the need for either the global custodian or subcustodian to re key the data into another format. This is known as 'straight-through' information processing and requires common technol-ogy standards at every stage along the communication chain. The global custodian is able to offer settlement activity reports to the investor in either hard copy form or by data transmitted electronically to the investor's PC link. Electronic reporting provides the investor with the opportunity to extract only the information that is required. This is achieved by transferring the data from the custodian's *Securities Movement and Control* (SMAC) system into the investor's proprietary computer system.

Through the use of spreadsheet software, the investor is able to sort the information in any order, eg, all trades on a particular settlement date, all trades in a particular secu-rity number, etc.

It is important to note that custody is an integral part of the investment process and a high level of confidence in the security of safe custody is indispensable in meeting investor protection objectives of:

*   preventing misuse of investors' assets
*   safeguarding ownership rights.

For registered securities, the name of the investor is shown on the face of the certifi-cate and reflected on the issuing company's register of shareholders. Private investors who do not use the services of a custodian for safekeeping purposes may have their holdings registered in their own names. Whilst this has the advantage that the bene-ficial owner can be readily identifiable (ie, name on register), it does cause adminis-trative problems for custodians who are appointed to look after the shareholdings of many investors.

For example, all dividends, corporate actions, company announcements etc, will be sent directly to the shareholders' addresses, and not to the custodian. The custodian will arrange for its clients' registrable investments to be registered in the name of a nominee company established by it specifically for that purpose. Whether the shares are registered in the name of the investor or the nominee, making changes on the company share register can be a time-consuming process, especially in a certificated environment. Re-registration can take anything from a week up to several months to complete, depending on the particular country. It is important to differentiate between legal ownership and beneficial ownership. Whoever's name is on the register has legal ownership of the securities. In the case of a nominee's name, the beneficial owner is the underlying investor, as shown in the following table:

Whose Name is on Company Register?	Legal Ownership Held by:	Ownership Held by:
Investor	Investor	Investor
Nominee	Nominee	Investor

For book entry securities, there are no certificates; these will be reflected by entries on a ledger statement:

The nominee company becomes the legal owner of the investments and its name appears on the issuing company's register of shareholders. Beneficial ownership is implied in this situation and it is the custodian's responsibility to maintain accurate records of the underlying beneficial owners. There are two different approaches to the management of nominee holdings both of which provide a secure and effective custody environment. This can only occur so long as proper and continuous controls are operated by the custodian. Under the pooled nominee system or omnibus system as it is often referred to, where all investors' holdings are registered in the same name (eg, ABC Nominees Ltd), the entries on the share register and the certificates do not identify the actual beneficial owners. What are the advantages of pooling?

- Administration is simplified and risk of clerical error reduced
- The settlement process is made easier as any certificate(s) may be delivered from the pool so long as the total does not exceed the number of shares actually held for the shareholder at the time of delivery

- There is only one holding for the custodian to reconcile in respect of each issue (although there must be a subsequent reconciliation of this holding to the records of the underlying investors)
- It reduces the number of names that need to be maintained by the registrar on the company register
- It provides anonymity for the investors except in cases where disclosure is required in accordance with the Companies Act 1985 s.212.

What then are the disadvantages of pooling?

Although it is prohibited, there is the risk that a custodian with poor controls might use the shares of one investor to settle trades of another when there are delays in the settlement system.

- It is difficult to establish beneficial ownership in the absence of comprehensive and up-to-date records
- More time is required to allocate dividends, corporate actions proxy voting, etc, to individual investors.

We can also use *Individual Designation* or *Segregation*. Under a system of individual designation within a nominee name, individual beneficial owners are identified by the addition of a designation. This designation, which can be a unique reference rather than a name, will also be reflected in the issuing company's register. What are the advantages of individual designation?

- Beneficial owners are more easily identifiable from the company register and the share certificates
- Reconciliation of share holdings to investors' balances is more straightforward
- Time spent allocating dividends, etc, is reduced
- The risk of using the balance of one investor to settle the trades of another is reduced
- Individual designation will facilitate the process of establishing claims for securities in a default situation.

What then are the disadvantages of individual designation?

- There is the risk that the holdings of one investor might be incorrectly designated under the designation of another investor
- It might be unsuitable for a custodian with many holdings over a wide client base. This would make the administration of such a client base difficult to manage and costly to operate.

We have discussed already the importance of the reconciliation process. Securities reconciliation is a control that seeks to establish that balances of assets beneficially owned by one party agree with the balances in the same assets held on behalf of the beneficial owner by another party. The Rules require that all safe custody holdings of investments must be reconciled at least twice during a period of twelve months at intervals of approximately six months. FSA in the UK allow reconciliation on a rolling basis rather than at two points in time. In this case there are extra conditions which must be satisfied including:

- confirmation from an auditor that there are adequate internal controls
- additional records reflecting clients' entitlements from an issuer's perspective.

Positions which do not agree, or reconcile, are queried in order to establish the reasons why; these can range from clerical error, unsettled trades and unauthorised use/fraudulent misappropriation of the assets. Global custodians and their investors reconcile their positions by electronically matching their respective securities balances, outstanding trades and corporate action events and, in so doing, produce an exception report highlighting only those securities which require remedial action.

Both investor and global custodian require asset listings which can be available in hard-copy format or from the custodian's software. The information on the asset listings usually indicates:

- Investor account identification
- Security name
- Security identification number
- Quantity of securities (ledger and settled balances, outstanding receipts/ deliveries balances)

- Name of depository in which security is held
- Valuation in currency of security
- Valuation in base currency of investor.

We know that "corporate actions" is a collective term used to describe the entitlements of any securities holder. We also know that they can be divided into those which require no action from the investor (eg, a bonus issue) and those which do call for the investor to make a decision (eg, a rights issue). What are the issues and implications in respect of custody arrangements and what does the operations manager and his team need to understand about this? For the global custodian, as for the operations manager in the firm or client using the custodian, there are a number of issues to take into consideration when dealing with events that require the investor either to make a decision or take no action at all. Timing is a big issue. Disregarding the risk factors, a trade that fails to settle on time will eventually settle. There might very well be penalty interest to pay and possible delays in other related trades; the trade nevertheless still stands. The overriding factor in those cases which require a proactive approach in order to benefit from the corporate action is for all parties in the information chain to deliver instructions before the deadline expires. A missed corporate action is irretrievable and internal controls must be able to recognise this possibility. It is important to record details of corporate actions in the ledgers on the correct date to ensure that the fund is priced correctly.

We have already discussed the source of information and managers must recognise this is therefore important, in the context of time and procedures. The prime source of information covering registered securities is the issuing company or its agent. The global custodian has to rely on the subcustodian network to gather this information and pass it on with a minimum of delay and translated preferably into English.

Other sources of information are the numerous information vendors such as Reuters, *International Securities Market Association* (ISMA) updates and the financial press. However, these secondary sources become primary sources for bearer securities where the issuing companies are unable to communicate directly with their shareholders and bond holders. The quality of information can be poor with two or more providers giving different versions of the 'same' data, language problems and time delays being the main problems experienced. The amount of benefit due to an investor is determined by reference to the quantity of shares each investor holds on a record date. This record date is announced by the issuing company. The local market will establish a date (the *ex date*) which is used to determine whether the buyer or seller of shares is entitled to receive the benefit.

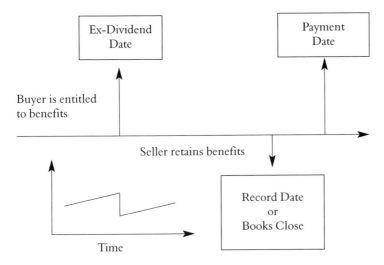

Figure 6.2   Cum & Ex Dividend
Source: the dsc.portfolio

A problem arises when a purchaser who has bought shares before the ex date (ie, is entitled to receive the benefit) does not have his name placed on the register before the record date. As the registrar is unable to recognise the new shareholder, the benefit is given to the previous shareholder, (the seller), even though he is not entitled to it.

The global custodian must make sure that entitlements are received in a timely basis to avoid lost opportunities in trading. There should therefore be a mechanism in place to ensure that the correct entitlements are received and, if not, claimed from the seller.

It is the global custodian's duty to provide as much information as is possible to enable the client to make the necessary decisions, to ensure that the information is accurate and to allow enough time for the client's instructions, where appropriate, to be relayed back to the company. As there is a variety of information types, it has not been easy for the global custodians to translate this into electronic message formats for the client. Instead, information on corporate actions has tended in the past to be sent by telex and mail. This situation is changing as the quality of information from the overseas markets improves.

The investor will be given a deadline before which to convey any instructions to the global custodian and for the global custodian to pass them on to the local market.

This can cause a problem for the investor who might want to delay his decision until the last possible moment which will be the deadline stated in the local market rather than the global custodian's. In this case the investor's settlement department and the global custodian have to delay sending their respective instructions until the very last moment and, in so doing, risk missing the deadline.

The investor must accept full responsibility for a missed event if instructions are sent after the custodian's deadline. Global custodians must ensure that clients' instructions are passed on to the local market and also that the benefit is received in good time. Where appropriate, market claims must be made.

An ISSA working party at the 6th Symposium in May 1992 recommended that:

> "Standard messages be used and standard time frames be developed for various corporate actions. Distinctions need to be made between those requiring timely reaction by the client and those which involve a simple notification and no response.
>
> That the information must be provided electronically as well in hard copy form. A central body, either public or private and accessible to domestic and international bodies, must be designated as the official carrier of the data in each market.
>
> That international issues should be communicated in English as well as the local language."

Despite the above recommendation when it comes to things like proxy voting, with communication in a foreign language, possibly across different time zones, there is a danger that companies are not able to inform their shareholders in time to cast their votes or react to news about corporate actions concerning their securities.

For global custodians to act efficiently and effectively on behalf of their investing clients, timely information has to be received from the companies. It is necessary for the custodians to have highly skilled staff in order to:

• decipher and translate lengthy technical information, and

- reorganise it in such a way that the client can make a timely and informed decision on the options available.

To ensure that all clients' decisions are transmitted to the company, custodian banks' staff must:

- be aware of the deadlines given by the company
- inform the clients of these deadlines
- ensure that missing client instructions are chased up before the deadline, and
- know the length of time it takes to send instructions to the company by:
  - SWIFT
  - telex/facsimile
  - mail.

It is not difficult to see that with the advent of widespread foreign share ownership and cross-border settlement, it would be an advantage if there were:

- greater uniformity of information dissemination
- standardised timeframes
- reliable information databases with easy global access.

These databases and the data communication networks connecting them to the information suppliers and users would be well suited to serve cross-border proxy voting.

It is now universally accepted that all shareholders should have an opportunity to exercise their voting rights, even though many of them may not actually wish to cast their votes. Indeed, there are some countries which are now beginning to encourage a more pro active participation by shareholders in the affairs of the companies.

Proxy voting is not normally a widely debated issue and only in isolated cases (where, for example, there is an outside attempt to gain control of a company) does the subject get coverage in the press.

As a result of increased shareholdings by large institutional investors, investment and pension fund managers have shown a new interest in exercising their voting rights.

This is partly in response to expectations expressed by the various regulatory bodies and partly an apparent underlying desire to influence a company's business or information policy. Large cross-border investments are reinforcing this trend and there is a call for a mechanism that will permit the exercise of voting rights across borders with the same ease as found in the investor's home country.

Lets us consider the problems for non-resident investors. Whilst the interest shown by the investors is both positive and appreciated by the companies, it is rarely possible for the foreign investors themselves to attend shareholders' meetings in person due to the distances and costs involved. Procedures vary greatly from country to country because:

- there are different laws and traditions
- there are different types of securities.

By the very nature of the instrument, companies do not know the names of shareholders whose certificates are in bearer form. These holders can only be contacted:

- via the media, and
- by custodians who research relevant information.

Registered shareholders usually have to be advised by mail via the registrars and, if applicable, by the relevant nominee companies. In a number of countries there are equity-type instruments or shares which:

- prohibit non-resident investors from voting
- carry no voting rights (for example, preference shares - these will only carry voting rights if the company has failed to pay its preference dividend)
- have a split voting structure (for example, companies such as Great Universal Stores plc have both voting shares and non-voting 'A' shares listed on the London Stock Exchange).

Investors now are opposed to the issue of equity without votes or with restricted votes in the belief that all shareholders who bear the same level of risk should have an equal voice in the management of the business.

- different languages,
- time zones, and
- formal requirements, eg, a printed proxy statement.

As a consequence, and with few exceptions, custodian banks do not advise their clients of forthcoming general meetings abroad. Therefore, holdings of non-resident investors are as a rule not represented at these meetings, unless standing proxy instructions are permitted and have actually been given. In the long term, this may prove harmful to the functioning of the democratic principles in a free market economy. The system should enable all shareholders, whether domestic or foreign, to vote if they should want to.

Furthermore, the cost of voting should be kept low and preferably absorbed by the issuing companies.

Of crucial importance in custody is cash management as the movement of securities, and in particular the settlement of securities trades, is linked to the movement of the corresponding countervalue of cash. Cash must be found to cover purchases; proceeds of sales and income payments must be re-invested in some way or another.

The prediction of cash requirements (funding requirements) and the movement of cash itself is known as cash management. The performance of an investor's portfolio is made up of:

- profit (or loss) on trading activity
- yield of the portfolio through receipt of income.

If little attention is paid to cash management, then, together with poor settlement performance, the overall performance of the securities portfolio will be affected.

The problems that would be created should a global custodian fall into receivership should be considered. It has been established that the ways in which clients' non-cash assets are held by global custodians are sufficient for the liquidator to identify separately those assets which are beneficially owned by the clients, and those which belong to the global custodian. The position for cash assets is not so secure; owners of cash are considered by the liquidator to be unsecured creditors in the accounts of the bank (deposit taker, borrower or global custodian). It is, therefore, wise to deposit cash only with those organisations which are able to honour debts and repay loans as and when they fall due. An indication of this ability is provided by *credit rating* companies such as Moody's, Standard & Poors and Fitch IBCA. These organisations constantly monitor the banks and will upgrade or down grade the rating to reflect the changed situation. A bank with a rating of AAA is considered better able to honour all debts whilst a bank with a rating of B is considered to be rather more risky.

Investors can reduce this risk by, for example:

- implementing in-house rules that might allow exposure limits of say $10 million with an AAA-rated bank down to $5 million with an A-rated bank, and no exposure allowed to banks with a B rating or lower
- making sure that the cash assets are placed with a number of highly rated banks.

While this will help to reduce the levels of risk, there is a price to be paid in terms of requiring more sophisticated cash monitoring systems and the extra expense associated with transferring cash around the banking system.

The global custodians are aware of the problems involved and constantly seek new ways to keep the client's cash related business in-house.

Clients whose business generates cash in (mainly) one currency and who wish to enter into cross-border trading might prefer to operate with cash accounts in a single currency. They will arrange for all purchase costs, sale proceeds and income receipts to be exchanged (a forex trade) into their base currency as and when the need arises.

For the investor, the advantages are:

- the exposure to adverse foreign exchange rate movements is removed once the Forex trade has been executed
- with only one currency, the funding requirement calculations are simplified
- the investor is free to obtain the most advantageous exchange rates from the Forex market place
- cash reconciliation and control processes are more straightforward.

The disadvantages are:

- there will be extra Forex trading charges to consider over and above the securities trading commissions
- the securities trade settlements will no longer be on a DVP as the currency movements will take place independently from the securities movements. The risk of non-performance of the trade as a whole is greater than it would be for a DVP settlement
- for Forex trades dealt with counterparties other than the global custodian, the investor must give settlement instructions for the cash side in addition to instructions for the securities.

For the global custodian, the implications are:

- the relationship is not one of global custodianship as defined by ISSA
- all income receipts are exchanged into the base currency
- the global custodian will not necessarily be responsible for exchanging the purchase and sale amounts as the investor will look around the foreign exchange market for the best foreign exchange rates
- the global custodian will continue to settle trades in the relevant currency on a DVP basis (where applicable)
- the global custodian is under no obligation to offer CSDA as the transfer of securities occurs independently from the movement of the client's cash.

On the other hand a client may require multi-currency accounts. Multi-currency banking will suit those investors whose ordinary business activities generate cash flows in foreign currencies and/or who prefer to settle the securities trades on a DVP basis in the foreign currency. The cash funding requirements will be undertaken as a separate process.

For the investor, the advantages are:

- the securities trades benefit from DVP settlement
- the investor is able to take advantage of the global custodian's CSDA settlement service
- there are more options available in terms of subsequent use of the foreign currency balances.

The disadvantages are:

- the increased control and administrative burden as a result of operating many different currency accounts.

For the global custodian, the implications are:

- a more rounded custody and banking service can be provided to the client
- the need to exchange all income into the base currency is removed thus reducing the number of relatively small value Forex trades that must be executed.

Investors who actively manage their cash balances wish to reduce or eliminate the time that uninvested or uncommitted cash balances remain in non-interest bearing accounts. Cash balances will be transferred to deposit accounts or other financial products. Although this achieves the objective, it increases the administrative burden and becomes expensive to operate. The global custodians now provide interest on various currency accounts and thus help to cut down the number of cash movements across the accounts. The global custodian may offer to transfer automatically (or sweep) uninvested and uncommitted balances overnight from non-interest bearing accounts into interest bearing deposit accounts or *Short Term Investment Funds* (STIFs). This ensures that cash balances are being used in a more efficient manner.

Global custodians hold accounts in the same currency and/or multi-currency accounts for their clients. For interest calculations only the custodians can pool the balances by currency into one larger balance in order to attract a higher rate of interest or reduce the effect of some accounts being overdrawn. Global custodians are also able to offer a wide range of banking services including:

- Funds transmission systems that enables the client to transfer electronically funds covering clean payments ie, those not directly connected to a securities trade
- Treasury services that provide dealing facilities to purchase and sell foreign currency, place funds on deposit and draw down funds on loan.
- Screen-based dealing systems that some global custodians have now made available which allow clients to execute their smaller Forex deals without reference to a bank dealer. Clients are able to accept or reject the rates offered on the screen and, should the rate be acceptable, the transaction is immediately confirmed.

Withholding Tax (WHT) occurs when cash benefits paid by companies to their share-holders in the form of dividends are subject to local tax. This WHT is deducted at source with the shareholder receiving the net amount.

The rate of WHT is determined by the tax authorities of the country in which the company is based. With the increase in cross-border investment activity, investors are subject to different tax regimes. Tax reclaims must be made in the issuer's country of origin and they will be submitted by the global custodian on behalf of the client.

There is no standard global approach to tax reclamation in terms of the timing of claims and repayment. In 1990, ISSA Recommendation 5 addressed this problem by seeking to obtain treaty benefits in an efficient manner by recommending that:

1.   treaty rates should be applied at source
2.   documentation should be streamlined and standardised
3.   details of beneficial ownership should be given on an exceptional basis only
4.   processing should take place through one agency per country.

Efforts to improve the situation have been made by the global custodians at the high-est levels in the problem countries. Unfortunately, progress is sometimes slow in spite of the industry's efforts as the issue of tax can only be resolved at an international, governmental level.

The problem for non-resident investors is that the net income is additionally subject to further taxation in their own country, ie, the income is double taxed. Most gov-ernments have recognised issue as being unfair and allow most or all of the WHT to be reclaimed by entering into a *Double Taxation Agreement* (DTA) with other like minded governments. Governments enter into these agreements with other coun-tries in order to:

•   prevent income being taxed twice, *and*
•   render reciprocal assistance to prevent tax evasion.

WHT reclamation works along one of the following bases:

•   certain classes of income are made taxable only in one of the countries who are party to a DTA, eg, in the country of the tax payer's residence

- income is taxable in both countries but (in the case of UK residents) the overseas tax is allowable as a credit against UK tax.

Additionally global custodians offer investment accounting services which is the provision of a full range of reports which may include fully accrued, multi-currency valuations, performance measurement, investment analysis, at both detailed and summary levels. Reports may apply to a single portfolio or a consolidation of a number of portfolios.

The cash management for principal dealers positions is also crucial and will be managed in various ways including treasury functions within the bank. A whole range of reporting of asset positions, funding requirements, credit lines etc. needs to be managed efficiently and yet as we have already seen this relies of efficient settlement and information about settlement (on time, delayed etc) as well as timely instructions to move cash in and out of accounts and liaison with custodians or other parties.

Another important service involves pricing and valuation reporting. Prices of individual securities are obtained from a variety of external price feeds, such as Reuters or Bloomberg, and allow the calculation of market value. From this the investors' portfolios can be valued both in the currency of the security and the base currency of the investor. It is important that the pricing of securities is carried out accurately and at timely intervals so the fund's *Net Asset Value* (NAV) calculations can be performed. An incorrectly priced security will lead to an erroneous NAV with the consequence that compensation might have to be paid to unitholders of the funds.

Funds and investors will wish to constantly analyse the performance of the investments. Using pricing information the investments can be analysed in a variety of ways:

- by instrument type ie, equities corporate bonds international bonds, government bonds, convertible bonds, derivatives and cash and cash equivalents
- by industrial sector
- against a benchmark index
- by geographical location
- as a percentage of the portfolio that each security or its type, industrial sector and geographical location represents

- by a sensitivity analysis showing how changes in securities or country allocations affect the return on the portfolio.

The information provided allows the investor to evaluate the value of the securities by stock selection, markets and currencies. There are a number of external performance measurement companies who collect relevant data from investors or global custodians in order to determine how investor types compare with each other or against industry recognised indices. This is relevant, for example, for marketing purposes when fund managers hoping to win new business will state that they have outperformed the relevant index by, say, 2% when the average has been 1%.

As the investment performance of a security includes the income received and income due it is important to be able to track the investment income . This is especially important for debt securities for which income (interest) accrues on a daily basis until the payment is made usually annually or biannually depending on the security type and domicile. Equally foreign exchange creates a possible cost or gain to the portfolio. The risk of forex exposure needs to be managed and therefore the foreign exchange reporting for a fund is vitally important.

Forex transactions should be related back to the underlying securities trades or income receipts. Historical exchange rates and interest rates should be reported to allow the investor to check the actual rates obtained against the market closing rates.

There are also requirements for consolidated reporting. Investors might use two or more fund managers, because each has a particular specialist investment skill. If the fund managers use their own global custodian, the investors have the problem of consolidating a range of reports from the fund managers and their global custodians into one combined set of reports. To save the investors' time and effort in making the consolidation, one global custodian acts as recipient for the reports generated by the other global custodians and prepares the consolidated set of reports.

For dealers positions, *mark to market* (MTM) reports are generated for comparison and reconciliation to dealers profit/loss record. MTM is the revaluation of positions against a price representative of the current market. The price can be generated and published by an exchange or can be generated from a pricing model.

Custody is integral to the whole clearing and settlement process and will form an important part of each organisations overall procedures for their business. As such operations managers must ensure that they understand the role of the custodian and how the custodians impact on their particular firm. Likewise staff should be fully conversant with the services and structure of custodians so that they are aware of crucial issues like timings, instruction formats etc.

WORK SESSION

Consider the various operational issues and problems that the manager in a custodian faces. Compare these with the problems that the manager in a client of the custodian might face and how the custodian has influenced this by either creating the problem or helping to address it.

Part of custody is the comprehensive use of technology and in the next chapter we look at this important subject and how it affects operations in todays markets.

7

TECHNOLOGY

Nothing has changed so much in the financial services industry as technology. A relatively short time ago most processes and particularly those in operations were manual and paper intensive. It is still true today of some processes and certainly in some countries but in general terms the use of technology has automated not just operations processes, but trading, payments, passing of messages and instructions.

This move towards greater reliance on technology is not without its problems. Issues like reliability, security and capability are usually all significant for organisations. So too is cost and support for as we saw in the chapter on Concepts of Risk, system risk is a key one in the industry. However, at least today most people working in operations are at least in possession of some IT skills although true understanding of the systems being used may not be great.

So what are the technology issues for operations managers?

Well, the last point in the previous paragraph is one. Just what do we know about the systems being used? What is the scope of the system to meet the operational needs? Are procedures driven by systems or do systems fit in with the procedures? Next to people, systems and technology in general can be the weakest part of any operations function and here we are not just talking about performance but about total collapse of the operational process.

Far too many operations teams operate on systems that are apparently unreliable and incapable of handling the products being traded or systems that are "adapted" to handle activity they were never designed for. The cause is usually lack of investment or poor operations and/or technology management or both. The cause of technology problems can be many and often include corporate policy or lack of it, failure of operations managers and teams to understand the technology issues and failure of technology personnel to understand operations functions and needs. So one blames the other and vice versa and the end result is more problems and greater risk.

The reality of course is that technology is expected to provide the answer to everything when in fact the systems are only as good as the input into their design from operations. Here lies the operations managers real challenge, understand the technology needs for the procedures and processes and then manage the development of those systems with the IT area.

Of course, there are many different ways in which systems are operated. They may be one or a combination of the following:

- Systems developed and supported in-house by the IT team
- Systems bought in from an external supplier and supported in-house by the IT team
- Systems bought in from an external supplier and supported externally by the supplier

In some larger organisations, the in-house IT team may not be employed by the company. Mostly for reasons of the enormous costs associated with IT, the technology development and support may be outsourced to a specialist company.

Managing the IT relationship is crucial. Key projects like STP, automating key processes like trade input, reconciliation and client services are critical to the business. Design, choice, implementation and post implementation are critical stages and the operations manager must be certain that the result will be right. There will be pressure from the team, from clients and also from senior management to get the "solution" implemented and yet rushing in new systems or even system enhancements rarely proves beneficial. Technology is power and yet so often it is power that is not realised because of relationship issues, resistance to change, politics, budget, lack of knowledge of the system and a tendency to blame systems for what is actually nothing to do with the system.

You will gather that the operations manager must be realistic when it comes to technology, recognising its benefits, seeing the need to ensure that sufficient knowledge about technology and the specific systems used is available in the team and to the team. The relationship between IT and operations will be either a formidable asset to the business or a potential disaster, its up to the IT and operations managers to make it the former. This can be achieved by establishing operations representatives with responsibility to liaise with IT and to provide the business reasons for issues. At the same time they receive the technology viewpoint and relay that to the operations teams in terms they will understand. In many organisations this works well, in others it doesn't, and it shows!

The use of technology in driving the industry forward is immense. Without it, book-entry transfer would not be possible so dematerialised settlement would be difficult to have. The volume and diversity of business would in turn be impossible to handle and the globalisation of the industry would never of happened.

STP is a key project for most organisations and obviously relies heavily on technology and yet its successful implementation is also dependent on operations teams changing their skills sets and working practices to embrace technology. Managing this process is also a key responsibility for the operations manager.

Internet and intranet facilities are changing the whole face of clearing and settlement leading the way in offering standard delivery mechanisms and links between customers and brokers and custodians own networks.

The introduction of *Real Time Gross Settlement* (RTGS) and *Continuous Linked Settlement* (CLS) require connectivity and two way access to data.

Technology also embraces most of the key functions associated with operations including:

- Record keeping
- Accounts
- Valuations

- Position reports
- Netting
- Profit/Loss calculation
- Client service delivery (internet/intranet data access etc)
- Margin calculations (derivatives)
- Trade confirmations
- Messages
- Settlement instructions
- Payment instructions
- Management information
- Static data
- Risk management (limits etc)
- Reconciliation.

The effectiveness of the procedures and controls applied by the manager will determine the efficiency of the operations team. In turn, the systems used for each of these processes needs to be able to deliver the performance the operations manager needs.

Industry wide technology is also crucial to the overall clearing and settlement process. The impact of the G30/ISSA Recommendations on standard messaging formats and the use of international securities identification numbering (ISIN) allows transactions to be universally recognised and the details to be matched. Thus we use unique identifying numbering systems such as CUSIP (US), SEDOL (UK) etc. for securities.

The SWIFT system of electronic communication with standard *message types* (MTs) for various cash and securities transactions was developed by the *Society for Worldwide Interbank Financial Telecommunications* is one of the most reliable systems around and handles millions of messages between all the major players in the markets. Organisations like ISMA have reporting systems (TRAX).

Treasury operations teams rely heavily on systems capabilities for information on funding requirements, positions and cash movement. Various systems are utilised in different jurisdictions so we have *Trans-European Automated Real-Time Gross Settlement Express Transfer* (TARGET) system that handles the settlement of cross-border payments of the Euro. Other systems utilised include the *Clearing House Interbank Payment System* (CHIPS) in the US and *Clearing House Automated Payment System* (CHAPS) in the UK. Most people are familiar with another payment system widely used BACS and there are other retail funds transfer systems that are not typically used in the wholesale markets.

The whole process of fund management requires a range of critically important reporting and valuation processes enabling investors and trustees to track the performance of the fund and to see the value and price at which they can buy or sell the shares or units. The accuracy of the valuations is vital and therefore the source of the information is also vital. High quality pricing data available online and real time applied to accurate records of the assets in the fund is needed to complete the *net asset value* (NAV) calculations on which prices are based. For all types of funds from unit trusts to hedge funds any significant errors and the regulators will take action. For instance a mispricing of a unit trust can require compensation to be paid by the manager to the investor and must be reported to the Trustee and the regulator. Reporting to customers is also subject to regulatory requirements including content, frequency etc.

Another important technology issue the operations manager needs to be aware of is the use of technology in enterprise-wide risk information systems. Risk data is managed in organisations through systems that receive the data from the business areas and then process that data through, for instance, an Interface Layer to a Data Integration Engine and onward into a Data Warehouse from which key risk reports, exposure monitoring and integrated reporting is made.

The operations manager will be involved in both the input of data from their area and the receipt of data from the Data Warehouse in terms of management information.

In output terms the use of the MI by the manager is important as part of the ongoing performance measurement process. Reconciliation breaks, interest claims, volumes, error rates etc. are all fundamental indicators of performance. As far as input is concerned, well we have already stressed that the quality of data out of operations and into the enterprise-wide systems. "Rubbish in = rubbish out" may be an old expression but it is nevertheless true. Today the inability to maintain accurate records has significant regulatory and, in an increasingly competitive environment, business implications.

Technology risk also needs to be considered. Access to systems is obviously vital for operations personnel and yet any tampering with data in the system can create massive problems. Creating procedures that segregate people with access to parameters and static data in the systems from those using the systems helps to control the risk.

The maintenance of static data is crucial. The system output is driven from the static data on:

- Products
- Clients
- Calculations (formulas, prices, interest rates, exchange rates)
- Standard settlement instructions (SSIs)
- Limits
- Charges, fees and commissions
- Maturity, expiry and termination
- Corporate actions

Data control sections in organisations are often established to oversee static data, procedures and elements of risk control. This is logical given the importance of data and technology in the operations environment.

The operations manager therefore has many technology issues to consider. Technology is driving the industry forward and the competition in the industry at all levels and in all fields makes effective use of technology critically important. Many of the day to day problems that arise in operations are, or tend to be blamed on IT and clearly the operations manager must be able to assess the true situation. Many routine and essential functions require systems to have good static data so this is another area of immense importance. Processes like netting, margining and real time settlement that are becoming more and more standard in all types of securities and derivatives clearing and settlement need system capabilities within the users to make them effective. Understanding the requirements and delivering the in-house solution is the managers objective.

We cannot leave the technology chapter without returning the developments going on in the industry today. The impact of internet and intranet facilities from a trading point of view where for instance an increase in private client business was seen after brokers began offering internet dealing has been significant and will grow in significance in the global environment, opening up markets and increasing cross-border business. Also the so called "added value" services that can be provided to clients using the available technology is changing the role of the broker, bank, custodian creating the need for massive investment in systems or a strategic withdrawal from the operational function, in other words outsourcing core clearing and settlement.

Examples where this is found include fund administration services, centralised clearing of derivatives and the concepts of prime brokerage. Operations outsourcing and insourcing will I suspect be a significant issue in the markets for some time. Outsourcing does not mean an end to the operations function in the outsourcer but it certainly changes the role. Likewise the insourcing company has taken on a massive workload and responsibility where the performance is subject to *Service Level Agreements* and the technology capability and investment needed to ensure that performance is significant.

Technology is changing operations and, as it does so, the operations manager must also change the procedures and the role of the people to meet the new world whatever it may be.

8

REGULATION AND COMPLIANCE

Every body from banks and brokers to fund managers and global custodians and their clients must operate within the general laws of the countries in which they are based as well as complying with any regulatory obligations. We could fill a whole book on regulation in the UK let alone globally and then be faced with the fact that change is happening in regulation as elsewhere in the industry. Keeping up to date with the regulations and their impact and complying with them is not always easy.

For the some organisations like a global custodian, this can become a complicated exercise when entering into legal agreements with subcustodians based in different jurisdictions. Equally there are issues for brokers and banks operating for clients where assets and money must be kept separate from the firms money and assets. Operations staff are in the front line as they are dealing with the flow of assets and money that must be safeguarded and treated as per the rules and regulations of the jurisdiction concerned.

Not only must the rules and regulations as laid down by the country concerned be adhered to, but so must the rules and regulations of the exchanges and clearing houses involved in the various processes. The regulatory environments need to be understood by operations teams even though compliance departments will specialise in the regulatory requirements.

Let us review the regulatory structures in the UK and US, starting with the UK where there has been significant changes. The main regulator of the securities industry is the Financial Services Authority, formerly the Securities and Investment Board (SIB), which operates under the Financial Services Act 1986 (FSA 86) and the Financial Services and Markets Act 2000.

The changes to the UK regulatory structure have taken place in stages. The UK structure consisted of 10 Principles laid down by the FSA, 40 Core Rules and a system of Self Regulatory Organisations (SRO) and Recognised Public Bodies. These organisations were required to implement the Principles and Core Rules set out in their own rule books which had been drawn up to meet the specific needs of its members.

There were three SROs in the UK:

- Securities & Futures Authority (SFA)
- The Investment Management Regulatory Organisation (IMRO)
- The Personal Investment Authority (PIA)

Further change took place with the introduction of the Financial Services and Markets Act 2000, which created a single regulator in the UK, the FSA.

The FSA has acquired the regulatory and registration functions which were formerly carried out by the Self Regulatory Organisations (SROs) and other regulatory bodies as detailed in the table:

The Financial Services Authority	
Regulator	**Regulated Organisations**
Building Societies Commission (BSC)	Building societies
Friendly Societies Commission (FSC)	Friendly societies
Insurance Directorate (ID) of the Department of Trade and Industry	Insurance Companies
Investment Management Regulatory Organisation (IMRO)	Investment management
Personal Investment Authority (PIA)	Retail investment business
Registry of Friendly Societies (RFS)	Credit unions' supervision (and the registration and public records of building societies, friendly societies, industrial and provident societies and other mutual societies)
Securities and Futures Authority (SFA)	Securities and derivatives business
Securities and Investments Board (SIB)	Investment business (including responsibility for supervising exchanges and clearing houses)
Supervision and Surveillance Division (S&S) of the Bank of England	Banking supervision (including the wholesale money market regimes)

Figure 7.1   Regulatory organisations now directly under the regulation of the Financial Services Authority

FSMA 2000 and Statutory Instruments give powers to and impose obligations on the FSA which in turn creates rules and monitors behaviour of the regulated entities.

The Act legislates in relation to regulated activities and Section 22 describes these as being a range of specified activities in connection with a range of specified investments. These are:

1. Deposits
2. Contracts of Insurance
3. Shares
4. Bonds
5. Instruments giving entitlements to investments (example: warrants)
6. Certificates representing securities (example Depositary Receipts)
7. Units in collective investment schemes
8. Rights under a stakeholder pension scheme
9. Options
10. Futures
11. Contracts for differences

12. Lloyds syndicate capacity and syndicate membership

13. Funeral plan contracts

14. Regulated mortgage contracts

Clearly the power of the FSA is extensive and regulated activities include, dealing as a principal or agent, managing investments, establishing and running collective investment schemes or stakeholder pension schemes, deposit taking and custody.

The FSA has 11 FSA Principles and also Conduct of Business Rules and also lists Recognised Exchanges and Clearing Houses. It is imperative that these are fully understood by the operations manager and that the appropriate procedures and controls exist within the operations area to address the issues that arise. There are so many key issues that affect the operations teams and it is not possible to cover the role of the FSA in great detail in this book. Readers who wish to know more about the UK regulatory environment and anyone taking the Securities Institute examinations are urged to visit the FSA website, www.fsa.gov.uk or alternatively purchase a copy of *The FSA Regulatory Environment IAQ Workbook* available form the Securities Institute.

The 11 FSA Principles are;

1. Integrity - A firm must conduct its business with integrity

2. Skill, care and diligence - A firm must conduct its business with due skill, care and diligence

3. Management and control - A firm must take reasonable care to organise and control its affairs responsibly and effectively, with adequate risk management systems

4. Financial prudence - A firm must maintain adequate financial resources

5. Market conduct - A firm must observe proper standards of market conduct

6. Customers' interests - A firm must pay due regard to the interests of its customers and treat them fairly

7. Communications with clients - A firm must pay due regard to the information needs of its clients and communicate information to them in a way that is clear, fair and not misleading

8. Conflicts of interest - A firm must manage conflicts of interest fairly, both between itself and its customers and between a customer and another client.

9.   Customers: relationships of trust- A firm must take reasonable care to ensure the suitability of its advice and discretionary decisions for any customer who is entitled to rely upon its judgement

10.   Clients' assets - A firm must arrange adequate protection for clients' assets when it is responsible for them

11.   Relations with regulators - A firm must deal with its regulators in an open and cooperative way, and must disclose to the FSA appropriately anything relating to the firm of which the FSA would reasonably expect notice.

Source: FSA Handbook

Operations managers must liaise closely with the compliance department over what is required to comply with the rules and regulations.

Another important key piece of regulation is the *Investment Services Directive* (ISD) which sets out the criteria for firms from EU member states involved in the provision of certain types of financial services. A key element of the ISD is the provision of the single passport allowing a firm to carry on business throughout the *European Economic Area* (EEA) with a single authorisation. The ISD defines the investments for which the passport applies and consequently a firm may be involved in investment activity that is defined under FSA but not ISD and other business that is defined under both. The *Second Banking Co-ordination Directive* (2BCD) affords a similar passport system for credit institutions ie, banks.

Regulation in other major jurisdictions varies from that in the UK. In the United States, the *Securities and Exchange Commission* (SEC) and the *Commodity Futures Trading Commission* are key regulators with commissioners appointed by the President. In Japan the *Financial Services Agency* and the *Ministry of Finance* oversee the regulation of markets and participants. From the operations managers point of view, understanding the relevant regulation in each jurisdiction is crucial and as we have noted here there needs to be close liaison with the compliance department.

The following diagrams show the structure of regulation in the US.

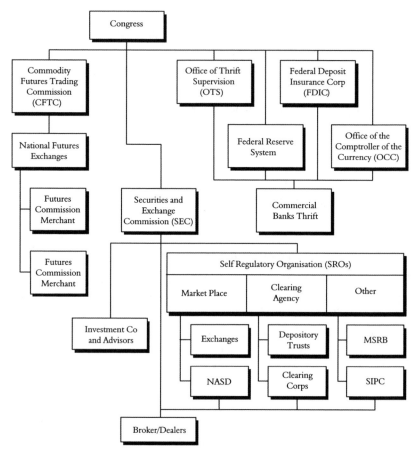

Figure 8.1   The structure of regulation in the USA
Source: ISSA Handbook

The strength of regulation is by no means standard around the world and operations managers need to be aware of this particularly where assets and cash are being held or moved. It is important for the reader of the book to research these international regulators, particularly those relevant to their firms business, and to make comparison between the regulatory structure and workings. However in general terms there are some key issues for the operations manager to address. These would include:

- Reporting requirements
- Client money and assets
- Money laundering
- Insider dealing.

The reporting requirements will range from activity reporting to large positions. The inference for the manager here is therefore that the record keeping function must be accurate and any amendments need to be made and if necessary the reporting also amended. Late reporting or failure to report amended trades can have significant repercussions.

With client money and assets, the requirements to adequately safeguard and segregate the assets is crucial. Calculating client money requirements and making shortfalls from own funds means that the manager must ensure that procedures and controls are effective and that one clients assets are never used to cover another clients shortfall or for principal activity. In the global context this will include ensuring that any assets or money held overseas is subject to the protection required or if this is not possible that the client is aware that the protection afforded is not to the standard of that in the UK.

Money laundering and insider dealing are serious issues, indeed criminal offences in some jurisdictions like the UK. More importantly there are responsibilities that each employee has particularly under the money laundering rules to report suspicious activity or simply concerns that something may be suspicious. The operations manager must make sure that at all times the team is aware of its collective and individual responsibility and the business must make sure that each employee is aware of how money laundering and insider dealing type situations can occur. The name of the firms *Money Laundering Reporting Officer* (MLRO) must also be known to all employees.

WORK SESSION

Compare the regulatory structure in the US, UK, Europe and Japan and note the key differences and the impact on the operations team.

Look at regulation in other markets like Australia, South Africa and China; what are the additional issues, if any that arise and then consider two emerging markets and again consider what operational issues arise.

9

CLIENT SERVICES

In a highly competitive industry the provision of high quality client services and customer relationship management is critical to all organisations.

There is choice in almost every field and with electronic processes switching counterparts is nothing like as difficult as in previous times.

Users or clients are also becoming more and more sophisticated in their use of the markets so expect better and more comprehensive services from their counterparts.

Everyone from systems suppliers to brokers to custodians is monitored for service levels, reliability, costs and value for money.

The key issues in respect of customer relationships include:

* The approach to client service and establishing a customer orientated culture
* The understanding of the client's organisational and business structure
* The risk impact of providing added value client services
* Measuring client risk
* Introducing controls and procedures to ensure performance standards
* Providing a competitive edge to the business
* Dealing with complaints.

These issues are of great importance. The ability of a business to retain and gain clients relies heavily on all aspects of customer relationship. The service provided out of the operations area will be judged by the client as part of the overall service provided by the organisation.

Managing and supervising customer relationships successfully revolves around:

- Choice of personnel
- Definition of the client service function
- Structure of the client service team or group
- Adequate training in key relationship skills
- Understanding of the client's business
- Policy and procedures for identifying and dealing with problems
- Relationship management policy.

Without the above it will be impossible for the manager/supervisor to monitor the service levels provided against the client requirements. As a result, the relationship management will be more difficult than it should be and there will be a real chance that the relationship may deteriorate and ultimately the client will move away. The diagram below shows a generic relationship between a fund manager and a derivatives clearing broker and illustrates the complexity, in terms of roles, responsibilities and potential problems areas.

Illustration of Relationships

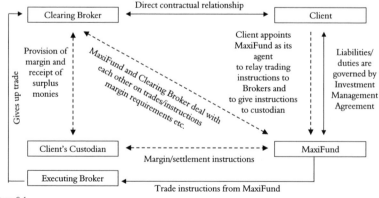

Figure 9.1

Providing a high quality client service is a full time role for a dedicated team of people. It is not therefore something that can be provided without a clearly defined policy and an adequate budget.

The customer relationship policy of the organisation must encompass both front office and operations such that the client is aware only of the "company" service. High degrees of personal and business skills are therefore required in the team.

This chapter will help to develop an understanding of the complex and crucial role of relationship management.

THE APPROACH TO CUSTOMER RELATIONSHIPS AND THE "CLIENT CULTURE"

Definition of "Client Culture": *A culture within and across an organisation that places the relationship with a client as the key to growth and profitability of the organisation, and one which is totally supported, resourced, implemented and managed by senior personnel in all areas of the business*

Both the approach to customer relationships and the establishing of a client culture are driven by market considerations as well as corporate policy. High on the agenda of business managers is the need for either market share or premier revenue generation from the client base. Both have fundamentally different implications for the way in which the client facing policy will be formulated. We must also add to this equation the market driven and dictated "customer service" issues and whether or not a particular business sector is service or profit driven. Today operational areas are just as much likely to be structured as revenue generators as service/administration providers. At one end of the scale there are organisations that have operations based client teams contributing significant revenue to the business by selling services and products independently from the sales teams. At the other end, client teams operating in "traditional" structures are providing the support and service levels that contribute to the company's core product. One might think there would be a significant variance to the approach to the relationships from two very different set ups and yet in reality there will be little if any difference.

Customer business is won or lost through for many reasons. A company failing to provide the client with the service they want and expect will lose that client whether or not they are revenue or cost based as a team. It is the service not the structure that is important and service depends on the culture possessed by the team. Most managers and supervisors would consider themselves customer orientated. How can it be otherwise when their function is to head up a team that serves others. However what we think and what the customer thinks are potentially two very different viewpoints.

Understanding the client, its business, its structure, its people and its objectives are vitally important. So too is the recognition that the client needs to believe that the service being provided is:

- As much for their benefit as the supplier
- Is supported by personnel that understand the clients profile
- Is able to offer innovative solutions to problems
- Can be expanded and adapted to meet the growth in the client's business
- Is "tailored" for the client.

Whether the client is in-house or external the above are all true. There is often a misconception about the importance of treating in-house relationships on the same basis as external client relationships. In many cases the principal activity is not only significant it is dependent on an efficient post transaction process to prevent unnecessary additional costs that will impact on profitability. There should be a clear policy that house "clients" receive a service in exactly the same way as an external client would expect to do so. It is not acceptable to treat the in-house client as "tame" and therefore provide a substandard service. If there is any reluctance to accept this viewpoint it may be worth reminding people that outsourcing is a very real option in today's markets!

So the client culture needs to be established as:

- A business objective for the organisation as a whole
- A function staffed by individuals that fully understand the concepts of and are totally focussed on client service
- Managed by an innovative and industry aware group
- Led by key managers interacting across the company.

Client satisfaction and support can be lost in a matter of months even when the relationship has been in existence for many years. Managing the relationship and service successfully is therefore crucial.

WORK SESSION

Marks and Spencer and Sainsburys are two examples where client loyalty has been lost at some point. What are the causes of the problems they have faced and what are the main issues in these two cases that can be applied to client service in the financial services industry?

We need to be able to define the service and establish relationships so that our personnel with direct client contact and, most importantly the rest of the operations team, understand the business need. It begs the question then, what is considered as Client Service?

One approach is to develop a service that can be a uniform product based on the basic settlement function that is "tweaked" to suit different types of client. This is reasonable as there are certain standard or core processes that will take place and there are common added value products like prime brokerage, fund administration and global clearing or by specific services like valuations, average pricing and single currency settlement. System supported services are important to many clients but not so important to smaller clients as say help and advice on new products, valuations and even regulatory issues. This is where the tweaking comes into play.

So the client service could be said to be: *"A standard settlement relationship that is enhanced by the provision of additional services that benefit the client"*

Managing the relationship and service successfully is therefore crucial. Relationships in any walk of life revolve around two key factors, *trust* and *compatibility*. There is no change to this when we look at the relationship between a bank or broker or custodian and their clients. The fundamental issues are about a belief that the relationship is mutually beneficial, is wanted and will be viewed as a long-term relationship.

The latter is very important. Today with so many system related issues and straight through processing high on the agenda, clients are seeking a counterpart that they will have a significant dependency on in terms of these system related services. It may therefore be tempting for a broker to believe that the client is "locked in" by the provision of technology related services. However that would be a mistake. Clients will move if the relationship sours, whatever the cost in terms of financial and disruption. The need to establish a monitoring process for the relationship for signs of problems is also a key element of managing the relationship. For instance a problem may be occurring only occasionally and yet is having an unseen, dramatic and damaging effect. For example a client is being inconvenienced and is losing confidence in their broker/bank as the counterpart. As we know in such a situation it is not inconceivable that the client may gradually move their business elsewhere and the counterparty may never be aware that it is the operations teams performance that is to blame.

Without adequate monitoring of performance and the relationship there is undoubtedly a strong probability that clients will be lost when it could and should have been avoided. The key issue is to develop the relationship in terms of both the team concept and the corporate concept. Clearly the day-to-day activities will be part of the relationship and it is here that the client culture we looked at earlier will be crucial. The minor issues and problems that may occur are being dealt with by the contacts in both parties operations. The way in which the operations area is structured will determine who is dealing with the client on the daily and ongoing basis.

So what are the main considerations for the manager?

- Structure of the Operations Team
- Who has responsibility for day-to-day client contact?
- How is the performance monitored?
- What are the escalation procedures for problems?
- Establishing a client liaison programme?
- Interaction and cooperation with the front office client team
- Identifying industry issues affecting or likely to affect the client
- Training the client facing and support teams in product awareness
- Analysing the competition
- Constantly reviewing, developing and refining the client service product.

Each of these issues is very much interlinked and forms the core subjects for customer relationship building and maintenance. We should consider them in turn.

STRUCTURE OF CLIENT SERVICES WITHIN THE OPERATIONS TEAM

Operations teams will all be different and yet will all be performing largely the same functions. The client facing team may be an actual team of people dedicated to the provision of client service. Equally it could be part of a middle office concept or designated people within a general settlements/clearing team.

RESPONSIBILITY

In most cases a client is looking for designated contacts at different levels. Daily contact is likely to be provided from a client team with a designated representative or account manager at the next level. Overseeing the whole client team may be a supervisor and team manager reporting to the operations manager.

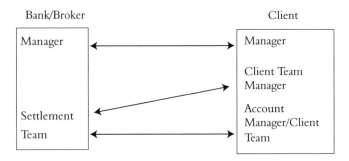

Figure 9.2   An illustration of the communication lines between a client (a) and a broker (b).

It is important that the day-to-day communication is separated from the senior management contact such that the people doing the processes deal with the majority of issues and problems. There can be a temptation, in the marketing of the services, for the more senior staff to offer to be the contact, a form of assurance of how important the client is viewed. Clearly this can be flattering for the client but is almost certainly going to be the beginning of a nightmare situation whereby every issue however minor is automatically routed to the Manager or Account Manager. There is a need for the responsibilities of each team member to be defined and for the contacts and their responsibilities to be explained to the client. This is important for external relationships but applies as well to the internal client. Clearly the client must not feel that the door is closed to them at any level but equally there has to be a logical order to the relationship. This may be included as part of a service level agreement if used.

Establishing the roles and responsibilities of the personnel on both sides of the relationship is fundamental to a workable and successful arrangement.

MEASURING PERFORMANCE

The combination of basic settlement processes and added value services makes measuring performance a complex exercise. As far as the basic settlement processes are concerned, performance is being monitored through workflow analysis. Our own benchmarking will provide the information that will highlight any potential problems the client might have experienced as a result. The unknown is what the client has perceived as a problem or what has occurred but, for whatever reason, it is not identified in the monitoring/benchmarking. It is important that within the client culture there is recognition of the need to understand the client's business. Only by doing this will the client facing team be able to appreciate what may be a potential problem for the client but is of no consequence to the broker. Another important factor in managing the relationship is to encourage open and frank discussion at all levels. Surprisingly, clients may not voice concerns as one might imagine. Therefore whilst the feedback from the team members and account managers is essential, it is still also imperative that the senior managers periodically meet with their counterparts at the client and encourage discussion of any concerns etc. Performance measurement and benchmarking is therefore a combination of:

- Management Information generated by workflow analysis
- Feedback from the client team
- Feedback from periodic senior manager client liaison meetings
- Internal feedback across the organisation.

The collation of the information, assessment and action must take place on a regular, possibly daily, basis and must be discussed with other client facing areas in the organisation. It is doubtful if many clients have only a single relationship with the organisation and to ignore the relationships with other non-derivative areas is foolhardy to say the least. We stated earlier that the client would look at the whole relationship with the counterpart, quite likely on a global basis, so feedback must be on a similar basis. It is important from a risk management point of view to share information and compare situations with respect to a counterpart. It is just as important to do so from a client service viewpoint because, as we have already noted, client service and customer relationship management is a team effort.

ESCALATION PROCEDURES

It is vital that the manager establishes a procedure whereby all issues are reported and documented and that appropriate action is signed off. This may well be by maintaining a "client log"

Issues covers such things as:

- Complaints
- Errors
- Failure to meet benchmark standard.

Action will range from written communication through to arranging a client meeting if the issue is serious. There may equally be a "no action" decision. By establishing the "client log" as a discipline in the team, the manager has every chance to pre-empt and prevent problems as well as providing a proactive management and response to the client in the event of a problem or failure to meet standard levels.

"Client logs" must be completed daily and record "no issues" as well as matters that require logging. It is important to set this "no issues" reporting as it can be used as a high profile means to measure performance.

CLIENT LIAISON PROGRAMS

The important question here is what are the liaison meetings to achieve?

WORK SESSION

Consider the following statements:

- Liaison meetings are only needed when a problem has occurred
- Liaison meetings are to allow a preamble before some kind of corporate entertaining
- Liaison meetings are to enable the broker to make a presentation on the developments to the services
- Liaison meetings are an informal opportunity to discuss issues.

Decide which of these statements you most agree with and then prepare an Objective List (internal use) and an Agenda (to be sent to the client) for such a meeting.

FRONT OFFICE CLIENT TEAM

Any client liaison program will need to be worked out with reference to the internal cooperation and relationship with the sales desk. Simple coordination of client meetings and information can be supplemented by regular meetings to discuss the client's activities, feedback etc. The successful development of the relationship with the client is conditional on the development of the relationship between operations and the sales desk team internally.

INDUSTRY ISSUES

Understanding the clients business, as we have stressed before, is essential to providing the kind of service the client will benefit from and appreciate.

The manager needs to create the environment where awareness of developments in the industry and in particular those that will have a significant impact on the client base, is obtainable.

This can be achieved through:

- Giving access to industry journals and web sites of relevant organisations such as the Association of British Insurers, Association of Unit Trust and Investment Funds (AUTIF) etc.
- Being members of industry associations
- Nominating people for membership of committees and working parties.

The ability of team members at all levels to discuss business issues with clients counts towards creating the desired professional image.

Training the Team

There is a constant need for training in client teams.

This training encompasses not only relevant business skills but personal skills such as languages as well. Part of the manager's role will be to establish coordinated structured training programs for client facing teams.

ANALYSING COMPETITION

Clients will inevitably make comparisons between the services available from brokers. They will analyse the latest developments in technology based services, costs, innovative services like OTC pricing, clearing etc.

The manager must be prepared to establish a process to provide continuous monitoring of the market place, both domestically and internationally.

This monitoring will feed into the ongoing development of the services.

DEVELOPING THE SERVICE

There can be a danger that a client team is set up with adequate resource, good levels of activity from quality clients and suitable procedures. Then business expands, clients increase in number and demands and the service is under pressure. This leads to problems, reputation damage and ultimately loss of business. This is perhaps an obvious observation and yet it can happen quickly if there is no planning and development of the service by the manager. This planning can be achieved by creating a business plan for the service encompassing:

- Products to be offered
- Products to be developed
- Personnel development
- Technology development
- Client business awareness
- Relationship management
- Performance measurement.

Such plans should cover the short, medium and long term and should not be a "wish list" but a carefully thought out plan including costs, revenue and risk management analysis.

WORK SESSION

Consider what would be needed from operations to support a Prime Brokerage product and also what a user of the product would expect from the Prime Broker.

WHAT ARE THE POTENTIAL PROBLEMS IN CUSTOMER RELATIONSHIPS?

There are numerous potential problems ranging from minor issues to full blown complaints. Identifying and dealing with each is the key to the successful relationship management.

If we assume that problems will fall into various categories we might come up with a matrix like the one below:

Category	Probable Source or Cause
Incorrect data	System problems, human error
Delayed data	System problems
Late settlement	Incorrect instructions
Missed corporate actions	Human error
Failure to respond to query	Human error
Argument over process or procedure	Personality clash
Interest Claim	Delayed settlement/incorrect data
Problems with "give ups"	Poor communication/human error

Figure 9.3   An illustration of the types of problems that can occur between a client and a broker and why they might occur

Any of the above can be minor or major issues and can occur because of either the broker or the client or both. It may also be the fault of an agent (internal/external) such as custodians, clearing agents, executing brokers etc.

Clearly the "give up " process offers scope for problems, so does the potential for a personality clash, although in the latter case active management of the client team should avoid an account manager being unsuited to the client.

Communication is often at the heart of many problems. It may be internal or external or both where the breakdown occurs.

Either way it needs to be stressed to the team that communication is vitally important to the efficient operation of the service.

The timing of any response is also vital. It is quite possible to pre-empt an issue becoming a problem simply by advising the client if say a system problem is likely to delay data.

MANAGING RISK WITHIN THE CUSTOMER RELATIONSHIP

Whilst the provision of a high quality client service is the objective of the team, doing so in a controlled manner is the overriding goal.

It is not good enough to take decisions on matters with a view to not upsetting the client. Avoiding unnecessary and contentious actions is fine only if there is no inherent risk, and where there may be a risk, that action is cleared at the highest level.

The manager has the responsibility for maintaining a good working relationship with the client in an environment that reflects the regulatory requirements and risk parameters of the organisation.

Offering client services like global clearing is exposing the organisation to certain risks over and above that for its normal business.

It is important to accept that client business is a counterpart risk and the added value services offered as part of the client package are increasing that risk.

The controls and procedures put in place by the manager to protect the organisation from such risk must form the basis of the customer relationship. Only in very exceptional cases or where there is realistically little or no risk in waiving a control, can such a decision be acceptable.

A client pressurising the broker to waive those controls in any other circumstance is unacceptable, whoever that client may be. Likewise, client service personnel cannot have the authority to waive controls and the manager should only authorise such a decision after first clearing it with the group risk managers.

If enforcing the procedure means that a client moves elsewhere, then that is a risk the manager must take after fully consulting with the client, the sales desk and the risk manager.

Consider the following potential situations:

1. Client fails to pay a derivative margin call on due day and due day + 1 citing problems at the custodian but says they will definitely settle tomorrow
2. Client fails to sign and return swap confirmation sent out ten days ago
3. Client needs to withdraw a maturing Treasury Bill which is collateral for a stock borrowing and promises to replace it with a new one next day
4. Client cannot provide the booking for a contingent trade in UK equities and US equities as the fund managers have not completed the order.

WORK SESSION

Consider the implications of the above situations and decide on the course of action you, as the manager would take.

CLIENT VISITS

We looked earlier at the client liaison visit and the objectives such a visit should have. Other important issues surround the communication with the sales desk and other client groups within the organisation over planned visits. It hardly inspires a positive image when the client receives two visits, sales desk and operations, on the same day from the same counterpart. This is particularly the case if the two teams are not aware that each other are making the visit.

In this chapter we have looked at an overview of customer relationships, a key area of the operations managers role. Successfully managing this area will depend on the choice of people, the policy on the service products and support and the constant monitoring of performance, industry initiatives and developments and changes to the business profiles of individual clients.

Years of building reputation and creditability can be destroyed in a very short space of time. The managers must convey this to ALL the team and make it especially clear to the client services team that they are nothing without the support and skills of the rest of the team. Likewise a super support team are wasted if the client service team cannot retain and gain new clients. Building a successful customer orientated operations team takes patience and often considerable tact. It needs to be managed and developed with drive and innovation allied to discipline and attention to detail. Over selling the services will lead to problems, under resourcing the structure will also cause problems. Failure to have adequate procedures and controls and to oversee the relationship management will be disastrous.

10

OPERATIONS IN THE FUTURE

Nothing stays the same for long. It is a fact all of us in the financial services industry know to be very true, at least over the last twenty years or so. We have already seen in the previous chapters just how much change is currently happening and indeed some of the change that will happen in the future.

As we move towards more automation in the markets, centralised clearing and dematerialisation in the clearing processes, so the straight-through processing (STP) projects will become complete. These STP projects will deliver greater capacity, which will be filled by new products and increased use of existing products.

Probably the biggest challenge the operations manager faces moving forward however is the conversion of teams, processes and procedures from various levels of paper and manual processes to more client focussed and risk management functions. Overcoming the natural resistance to change is going to be a significant challenge particularly as there will be no "big bang" change but rather a change over time.

As the operation function becomes more professional and more high profile in its contribution to successful businesses, demands for greater and more diverse skills will arise. The manager needs to focus today on what will be needed in the future. Training and re-training individuals and teams to meet new requirements will obviously be a large part of the manager's role.

As the regulatory environments evolve, other challenges will occur both in terms of ensuring that the operations function is complying with the environment, but also in the need to maintain the levels of competency laid down.

The ever-increasing competitiveness in the industry will also create challenges. As less paper, faster settlement becomes the norm so the ability to provide new, innovative and reliable client services products from operations to supplement the products offered from the front office will become absolutely critical.

Systems as always will be central to the whole operations environment and the STP projects, internet/intranet settlement and client services facilities will be at the heart of the future operations set up.

As the industry moves forward the increasing demands for high skilled teams, ever more sophisticated systems to support increased volumes in diverse products and more complex client services products will lead to reviews of the merits of in-sourcing and out-sourcing. The custody industry has seen changes in the past caused by reassessment of viability as costs increased and revenue was squeezed. Many organisations opted to close their custody operations and it is likely that similar decisions will be taken by banks and fund management companies in the future.

We know that operational risk is now a significant subject in the industry. The importance of the subject will not diminish, especially in the light of the terrible events on the 11th September 2001 that so graphically illustrated the need for disaster recovery sites, but also showed just what a valuable commodity people are. In fact risk and the people management process are the challenges of the future in a changing world full of uncertainty. This includes recognising the value of everyone in the process chain in terms of not only their qualities that may be lost, but also in the immense ability of people to overcome a setback however big and win through because of the sheer willpower, pride and skills. Harnessing the talents of people and developing people will become a greater part of the operations managers brief in years to come. More sophisticated use of more complex and varied products coupled with shortening settlement cycles, STP, more demanding regulatory environments and greater emphasis on the delivery and use of client service products will create demands on people and systems the like of which we do not currently see.

Today there are many demands on individuals, systems and managers. At present, the problems and challenges stem from the evolution of clearing and settlement, an evolution that is neither consistent nor complete in many parts of the industry and certainly not worldwide.

The GSCS Benchmarks show us that the standards are rising but, that there is still a gulf between different countries, markets and products. Centralising clearing will undoubtedly address this but that will not happen uniformly whilst politics and vested interests are at work. The next ten years will see central counterparty clearing for all major products traded on-exchange and for many over-the-counter products as well. The greater independent risk management afforded by the use of a central counterparty will need to be mirrored by enhanced risk management in the banks, brokers and institutional clients. Private client business, either in the private banking/broking fields or through the internet shops will no doubt continue to grow. Operational risk capital will occupy thoughts, minds and not a little money and faster settlement, seamless delivery of information, less time to analyse and resolve errors, highly competitive and pressurised environments will all be there for the manager to manage.

With so much change, much of it to the fundamental structures of the markets, it will probably be the pace of that change that will present the greatest challenge for the operations manager. If we consider how London has relatively rapidly moved from a large domestic run market to one that is now dominated by foreign banks, it is argued in some quarters that the markets themselves may move out of the UK. On the plus side for London is of course the huge pool of expertise here plus the fact that many of the "foreign" owners are in fact American and the infrastructure including language suits them. However business is global and if the operations arms of foreign banks are to have any significant role in London rather than say Frankfurt, operations teams have to be developed that are versatile, innovative, highly trained and delivering a consistently high standard. The need to be cost effective goes without saying.

The challenge for the future then is managing rapid change and re-training and equipping operations teams. The market downturn through the latter part of 2000 has not helped the case for high expenditure to develop and deliver the operations teams of tomorrow. Managers may be used to tight budgets but in this case they must fight the finance director by developing coherent and cost effective policies and business plans to take operations to the next stage.

Within those business plans must be the way in which operations delivers critical input to the business.

This can be illustrated by focussing on key issues such as:

- Capital for operational risk
- Delivery of client added value services
- Increased risk management role.

Outsourcing is an inevitable option for senior management in most organisations but equally insourcing can be a counter option.

Other key factors will be those that all managers and supervisors have faced before such as managing expectations, balancing skill sets, responding to business flows and forging relationships with counterparties.

The future, like the present will be a huge challenge, but then again professionals relish challenge.

Glossary

30/360

Also 360/360 or 30(E)/360. A day/year count convention assuming 30 days in each calendar month and a 'year' of 360 days; adjusted in America for certain periods ending on 31st day of the month (and then sometimes known as 30(A)/360).

AAA

The highest credit rating for a company or asset – the risk of default is negligible.

Accrued Interest

Interest due on a bond or other fixed income security that must be paid by the buyer of a security to its seller. Usual compensation: coupon rate of interest times elapsed days from prior interest payment date (ie, Coupon date) up to but not including settlement date.

Actual Settlement Date

Date the transaction effectively settles in the clearing house (exchange of securities eventually against cash).

Add-on

In capital adequacy calculations, the extra capital required to allow for the possibility of a deal moving into profit before a mark-to-market calculation is next made.

Affirmation

Affirmation refers to the counterparty's agreement with the terms of the trade as communicated.

Agent

One who executes orders for or otherwise acts on behalf of another (the principal) and is subject to its control and authority. The agent takes no financial risk and may receive a fee or commission.

Alternative Investment Market (AIM)

Second tier of market run by the London Stock Exchange.

American Depository Receipt (ADR)

Document giving the owner rights to UK shares. They are effectively bearer documents.

American Style Option

The holder of the long position can choose to exercise the position into the underlying instrument until the expiry day.

AMEX

American Stock Exchange.

Amortisation

Accounting procedure that gradually reduces the cost value of a limited life asset or intangible asset through periodic charges to income. The purpose of amortisation is to reflect the resale or redemption value. Amortisation also refers to the reduction of debt by regular payments of interest and principal to pay off a loan by maturity.

Ask price

Price at which a market maker will sell stock. Also known as the offer price.

Asset Allocation

The use of derivatives by a fund manager, to immediately gain or reduce exposure to different markets.

Asset Backed Securities

Debt obligations that pay principal and interest; principal only or interests only; deferred interest and negative interest using a combination of factors and rate multipliers. The issues are serviced by multiple vendors that supply the necessary data to make the corresponding payments.

Assets

Everything of value that is owned or is due: fixed assets (cash, buildings and machinery) and intangible assets (patents and good will).

Assignment

The process by which the holder of a short option position is matched against a holder of a similar long option position who has exercised his right.

ASX

Australian Stock Exchange.

Authentication agent

A bank putting a signature on each physical bond to certify its genuineness prior to the distribution of the definitive bonds on the market.

Authorisation

Status required by the Financial Services and Markets Act 2000 for any firm that wants to conduct investment business.

Authorised Unit Trust

Unit trust which meets the requirements of the Financial Services Authority to allow it to be freely marketable.

Bank – commercial

Organisation that takes deposits and makes loans.

Bank – merchant

Organisation that specialises in advising on takeovers and corporate finance activities

Bank of England

The UK's central bank which undertakes policy decided by the Treasury and determines interest rates.

Bankers' acceptance

Short term negotiable discount note, drawn on and accepted by banks which are obliged to pay the face value amount at maturity.

GLOSSARY

Bargain

Another word for a transaction or deal. It does not imply that a particularly favourable price was obtained.

Base Currency

Currency chosen for reporting purposes.

Basis (Gross)

The difference between the relevant cash instrument price and the futures price. Often used in the context of hedging the cash instrument.

Basis (Value or Net)

The difference between the gross basis and the carry.

Basis Point (B.P.)

A change in the interest rate of one hundredth of one per cent (0.01%). One basis point is written as 0.01 when 1.0 represents 1%.

Basis Risk

The risk that the price or rate of one instrument or position might not move exactly in line with the price or rate of another instrument or position which is being used to hedge it.

BBA

British Bankers' Association.

Bear

Investor who believes prices will fall.

Bearer Document

Documents which state on them that the person in physical possession (the bearer) is the owner.

Benchmark Bond

The most recently issued and most liquid government bond.

Beneficial Owner

The underlying owner of a security who has paid for the stock and is entitled to the benefits of ownership.

Bid

The price or yield at which a purchaser is willing to buy a given security.

To quote a price or yield at which a purchaser is able to buy a given security.

Bilateral Netting

A netting system in which all trades executed on the same date in the same security between the same counterparties are grouped and netted to one final delivery versus payment.

Bill of exchange

A money market instrument.

BIS

Bank for International Settlements.

Block Trade

A purchase or sale of a large number of shares or dollar value of bonds normally much more than what constitutes a round lot in the market in question.

Bond

A certificate of debt, generally long-term, under the terms of which an issuer contracts, inter alia, to pay the holder a fixed principal amount on a stated future date and, usually, a series of interest payments during its life.

Bonus Issue

A free issue of shares to a company's existing shareholders. No money changes hands and the share price falls pro rata. It is a cosmetic exercise to make the shares more marketable. Also known as a capitalisation or scrip issue.

Book Entry Transfer

System of recording ownership of securities by computer where the owners do not receive a certificate. Records are kept (and altered) centrally in 'the book'.

Break

A term used for any out-of-balance condition. A money break means that debits and credits are not equal. A trade break means that some information such as that from a contra broker is missing to complete that trade.

Bretton Woods Agreement

An agreement that set a system of exchange rate stability after World War II, with all member currencies having a par value pegged to the US$, allowing a 1% variance. This was agreed by major economists from 44 countries. The International Monetary Fund and the World Bank was agreed to be set up at this conference.

Broker/Dealer

Any member firm of the Stock Exchange except the specialists which are GEMMs and IDBs.

Broken date

A maturity date other than the standard ones normally quoted.

Broken period

A period other than the standard ones normally quoted.

Broking

The activity of representing a client as agent and charging commission for doing so.

Bull

Investor who believes prices will rise.

Buying In

The action taken by a broker failing to receive delivery of securities from a counter-party on settlement date to purchase these securities in the open market.

CASCADE

Name of the settlement system used by Clearstream for German equity settlement.

Calendar spread

The simultaneous purchase (or sale) of a futures or option contract for one date and the sale (or purchase) of a similar futures contract for a different date. See spread.

Call Option

An option that gives the seller the right, but not the obligation, to buy a specified quantity of the underlying asset at a fixed price, on or before a specified date. The buyer of a call option has the obligation (because they have bought the right) to make delivery of the underlying asset if the option is exercised by the seller.

Call Spread

The purchase of a call option coupled with the sale of another call option at a different strike, expecting a limited rise or fall in the value of the underlying.

Callable Bond

A bond that the issuer has the right to redeem prior to maturity by paying some specified call price.

Capital Adequacy

Requirement for firms conducting investment business to have sufficient funds.

Capital Markets

A term used to describe the means by which large amounts of money (capital) are raised by companies, governments and other organisations for long term use and the subsequent trading of the instruments issued in recognition of such capital.

Capitalisation Issue

See Bonus Issue.

Cash Market

A term used to describe the market where the cash asset trades, or the underlying market when talking about derivatives.

Cash Sale

A transaction on the floor of the stock exchange which calls for delivery of the securities that same day. In "regular way" trades, the seller delivers securities on the fifth business day.

Cash Settlement

In the money market a transaction is said to be made for cash settlement if the securities purchased are delivered against payment on the same day the trade is made.

CBOT

Chicago Board of Trade.

CEDCOM

Communication system operated by Clearstream.

Central Securities Depository

An organisation which holds securities in either immobilised or dematerialised form thereby enabling transactions to be processed by book entry transfer. Also provides securities administration services.

Certificate of Deposit

A money market instrument.

CFTC

The Commodities and Futures Trading Commission, (United States).

Chaps

Clearing House Automated Payment System – clearing system for Sterling and Euro payments between banks.

Cheapest to Deliver

The cash security that provides the lowest cost (largest profit) to the arbitrage trader; the cheapest to deliver instrument is used to price the futures contract.

CHIPS

Clearing House Interbank Payments System – clearing system for US dollar payments between banks in New York.

Clean Price

The total price of a bond less accrued interest.

Clearance

The process of determining accountability for he exchange of money and securities between counterparties to a trade: clearance creates statements of obligation for securities and/or funds due.

Clearance Broker

A broker who will handle the settlement of securities related transactions for himself or another broker. Sometimes, small brokerage firms may not clear for themselves and therefore employ the services of an outside clearing broker.

Clearing

The centralised process whereby transacted business is recorded and positions are maintained.

Clearing Organisation

The clearing organisation acts as the guarantor of the performance and settlement of contracts that are traded on an exchange.

Clearstream

CSD and clearing house based in Luxembourg and Frankfurt.

Close ended

Organisations such as companies which are a certain size as determined by their share capital.

Closing Day

In a new bond issue, the day when securities are delivered against payment by syndicate members participating in the offering.

Closing Trade

A bought or sold trade which is used to partly offset an open position, to reduce it or to fully offset it and close it.

CME

Chicago Mercantile Exchange.

CMO

Central Moneymarkets Office – clearing house and depository for UK money markets.

Collateral

An acceptable asset used to cover a margin requirement.

Commercial paper

A money market instrument.

Commodity Futures

These comprise five main categories; agriculturals eg, wheat and potatoes, softs eg, coffee and cocoa, precious metals eg. gold and silver, non-ferrous metals eg, copper and lead, and energies eg, oil and gas.

Common Stock

Securities which represent ownership in a corporation. The two most important common stockholder rights are the voting right and dividend right. Common stockholder's claims on corporate assets are subordinate to those of bondholders preferred stockholders and general creditors.

Compliance Officer

Person appointed within an authorised firm to be responsible for ensuring compliance with the rules.

Compound interest

Interest calculated on the assumption that interest amounts will be received periodically and can be re-invested (usually at the same rate).

Conduct of Business Rules

Rules required by FSA 1986 to dictate how firms conduct their business. They deal mainly with the relationship between firm and client.

Confirm

An agreement for each individual OTC transaction which has specific terms.

Continuous Net Settlement

Extends multilateral netting to handle failed trades brought forward – see *multilateral netting*.

Contract

The standard unit of trading for futures and options. It is also commonly referred to as a "lot".

Contract for Difference

Contract designed to make a profit or avoid a loss by reference to movements in the price of an item. The underlying item cannot change hands.

Contract Note

Legal documentation sent by securities house to clients providing details of a transaction completed on their behalf.

Convertible Bond

Security (usually a bond or preferred stock) that can be exchanged for other securities, usually common stock of the same issuer, at the option of the holder and under certain conditions.

Core Rules

40 rules written by FSA under the three-tier approach, to be universally applicable. Dedesignated in November 1994.

Corporate Action

One of many possible capital restructuring changes or similar actions taken by the company, which may have an impact on the market price of its securities, and which may require the shareholders to make certain decisions.

Corporate Debt Securities

Bonds or commercial papers issued by private corporations.

Corporate Finance

General title which covers activities such as raising cash through new issues.

Correlation

Refers to the degree to which fluctuations of one variable are similar to those of another.

Cost of carry

The net running cost of holding a position (which may be negative) eg, the cost of borrowing cash to buy a bond, less the coupon earned on the bond while holding it.

Counterparty

A trade can take place between two or more counterparties. Usually one party to a trade refers to its trading partners as counterparties.

Coupon

Generally, the nominal annual rate of interest expressed as a percentage of the principal value. The interest is paid to the holder of a fixed income security by the borrower. The coupon is generally paid annually, semi-annually or, in some cases quarterly depending on the type of security.

Credit Creation

Expansion of loans which in turn expands the money supply.

Credit Derivatives

Credit derivatives have as the underlying asset some kind of credit default. As with all derivatives, the credit derivative is designed to enable the risk related to a credit issue, such as non-payment of an interest coupon on a corporate or sovereign bond, or the non-repayment of a loan, to be transferred.

Credit risk

The risk that a borrower, or a counterparty to a deal, or the issuer of a security, will default on repayment or not deliver its side of the deal.

CREST

The organisation in the UK that holds UK and Irish company share in dematerialised form and clears and settles trades in UK and Irish company shares.

CRESTCo

Organisation which owns CREST.

CREST member

A participant within CREST who holds stock in stock accounts in CREST and whose name appears on the share register. A member is their own user.

Crest sponsored member

A participant within CREST who holds stock in stock accounts in CREST and whose name appears on the share register. Unlike a member, a sponsored member is not their own user. The link to CREST is provided by another user who sponsors the sponsored member.

Cross Border Trading

Trading which takes place between persons or entities from different countries.

Covered Writing

The sale of call options but the seller owns the stock which would be required to cover the delivery, if called.

Cum-dividend

With dividend.

Currency Exposure

Currency exposure exists if assets are held or income earned, in one currency while liabilities are denominated in another currency. The position is exposed to changes in the relative values of the two currencies such that the cost of the liabilities may be increased or the value of the assets or earning decreased.

Currency Futures

Contracts calling for delivery of a specific amount of a foreign currency at a specified future date in return for a given amount of say US Dollars.

CUSIP

The committee on Uniform Securities Identification Procedures, the body which established a consistent securities numbering system in the United States.

Custodian

Institution holding securities in safekeeping for a client. A custodian also offers different services to its clients (settlement, portfolio services...).

Customer-non-private

Customer who is assumed to understand the workings of the investment world and therefore receives little protection from the Conduct of Business Rules.

Customer – private

Customer who is assumed to be financially unsophisticated and therefore receives more protection from the Conduct of Business Rules.

D.K.

Don't Know. Applies to a securities transaction pending settlement where fundamental data is missing which prevents the receiving party from accepting delivery.

Dealer

Individual or firm that acts as principal in all transactions, buying for his own account.

Debenture

Another name for a corporate bond – usually secured on assets of the company.

Deferred share

A class of share where the holder is only entitled to a dividend if the ordinary shareholders have been paid a specified minimum dividend.

Delivery versus Payment

Settlement where transfer of the security and payment for that security occur simultaneously.

Delivery

The physical movement of the underlying asset on which the derivative is based from seller to buyer.

Dematerialised (form)

Circumstances where securities are held in a book entry transfer system with no certificates.

Depository Receipts

Certificate issued by a bank in a country to represent shares of a foreign corporation issued in a foreign country. It entitles the holder to dividends and capital gains. They trade and pay dividend in the currency of the country of issuance of the certificate.

Depository Trust Company (DTC)

A US central securities depository through which members may arrange deliveries of securities between each other through electronic debit and credit entries without the physical delivery of the securities. DTC is industry owned with the NYSE as the majority owner. DTC is a member of the Federal Reserve System.

Derivative

A financial instrument whose value is dependent upon the value of an underlying asset.

Direct Market Participant

A broker, broker/dealer or any direct member of an exchange.

Dirty Price

The total price of a bond including accrued interest.

Disclaimer

A notice or statement intending to limit or avoid potential legal liability.

Discount Securities

Non-interest bearing short term securities that are issued at discount and redeemed at maturity for full face value.

Deutsche Börse

The German Stock Exchange.

Dividend

Distribution of profits made by a company if it chooses to do so.

Dividend Yield

The dividend expressed as a percentage of the share price.

Diversification

Investment strategy of spreading risk by investing the total available in a range of investments.

Domestic Bond

Bond issued in the country of the issuer, in its country and according to the regulations of that country.

Dow Jones Index

Main share index used in the USA.

DTC

Depository Trust Company – CSD for shares in the USA.

Duration

A measure of the relative volatility of a bond; it is an approximation for the price change of a bond for a given change in the interest rate. Duration is measured in units of time. It includes the effects of time until maturity, cash flows and the yield to maturity.

ECB

European Central Bank.

ECSDA

European Central Securities Depository Association.

EFP

Exchange of futures for physical. Common in the energy markets. A physical deal priced on the futures markets.

EUCLID

Communications system operated by Euroclear.

EUREX

German-Swiss derivatives exchange created by the merger of the German (DTB) and Swiss (SOFFEX) exchanges.

EURONEXT

An amalgamation of the Dutch, French and Belgium Exchanges.

Earnings per share (EPS)

The total profit of a company divided by the number of shares in issue.

Elective event

Corporate action which requires a choice from the security owner.

Electronic Order Book

The electronic order matching system used as the system for dealing in the shares which comprise the FT-SE 100 stock.

Emerging Market

Non-industrialised country with

- low or middle per capita income, as published annually by the World Bank,
- Undeveloped capital market (ie, the market represents only a small portion of their GDP).

Equity

A common term to describe stocks or shares.

Equity / Stock Options

Contracts based on individual equities or shares. On exercise of the option the specified amount of shares are exchanged between the buyer and the seller through the clearing organisation.

E-T-D

This is the common term which is used to describe Exchange Traded Derivatives which are the standardised products. It also differentiates products which are listed on an exchange as opposed to those offered Over-The-Counter.

ETF Exchange-Traded Funds

Passively managed basket of stocks that mirrors a particular index and that can be traded like ordinary shares. They trade intraday on stock exchanges, like securities, at market determined prices. In essence, ETFs are index funds that trade like stocks.

EURIBOR

A measure of the average cost of funds over the whole euro area based on a panel of 57 banks.

Euro

The name of the single European currency.

Euro-Commercial

Unsecured corporate debt with a short maturity structured to appeal to large financial institutions active in the Euro Market.

Eurobond

An interest bearing security issued across national borders, usually issued in a currency other than that of the issuer's home country.

Euroclear

A book-entry clearing facility for most Eurocurrency and foreign securities. It is owned by a large number of banks of North American and European origin and is managed by Morgan Guaranty Trust in Brussels.

European Style Option

An option which can only be exercised on the expiry day.

Exception-based processing

Transaction processing where straightforward items are processed automatically, allowing staff to concentrate on the items which are incorrect or not straightforward.

Exchange

Market place for trading.

Exchange Delivery Settlement Price (EDSP)

The price determined by the exchange for physical delivery of the underlying instrument or cash settlement for derivatives.

Exchange Owned Clearing Organisation

Exchange or member owned clearing organisations are structured so that the clearing members each guarantee each other with the use of a members default fund and additional funding like insurance, with no independent guarantee.

Exchange Rate

The rate at which one currency can be exchanged for another.

Ex-Date

Date on or after which a sale of securities is executed without the right to receive dividends or other entitlements.

Ex-dividend

37 days before interest payment is due gilt-edged stocks are made 'ex-dividend'. After a stock has become 'ex-dividend', a buyer of stock purchases it without the right to receive the next (pending) interest payment.

Execute and eliminate order

Type of order input into SETS. The amount that can be tracked immediately against displayed orders is completed, with the remainder being rejected.

Execution

The action of trading in the markets.

Exercise

The process by which the holder of an option may take up their right to buy or sell the underlying asset.

Exercise price (or Strike price)

The fixed price, per share or unit, at which an option conveys the right to call (purchase) or put (sell) the underlying shares or units.

Expiry date

The last date on which an option holder can exercise their right. After this date an option is deemed to lapse or be abandoned.

Ex-Warrants

Trading a security so that the buyer will not be entitled to warrants that will be distributed to holders.

Face Value

The value of a bond, note, mortgage or other security that appears the face of the issue, unless the value is otherwise specified by the issuing company. Face value is ordinarily the amount the issuing company promises to pay at maturity. Face value is also referred to as par value or nominal value.

Failed transaction

A securities transaction that does not settle on time; ie, the securities and/or cash are not exchanged as agreed on the settlement date.

Fair Value

For futures, it is the true price not the market price, allowing for the cost of carry. For options, it is the true price, not the market price, as calculated using an option pricing model.

Federal Reserve Book Entry System

CSD for US government securities.

Fill or Kill order

Type of order input into SETS. It is either completed in full against displayed orders or rejected in full.

Final Settlement

The completion of a transaction when the delivery of all components of a trade is performed.

Financial Futures/Options contracts

Financial futures is a term used to describe futures contracts based on financial instruments like currencies, debt instruments and financial indices.

Financial Services and Markets Act 2000

The legislation that created the single UK Regulator, the Financial Services Authority.

Financial Services Authority (FSA)

The agency designated by the Treasury to regulate investment business as required by FSA 1986. It is the main regulator of the financial sector and was formerly called the Securities and Investments Board (SIB). It assumed its full powers on 1st December 2001.

Fiscal Agent

A commercial bank appointed by the borrower to undertake certain duties related to the new issue, such as assisting the payment of interest and principal, redeeming bonds or coupons, handling taxes, replacement of lost or damaged securities, destruction of coupons and bonds once payments have been made.

Fiscal Years

These run from 6th April to 5th April and are the periods of assessment for both income tax and capital gains tax.

Fit and Proper

Under FSA 86 everyone conducting investment business must be a 'fit and proper person'. The Act does not define the term, a function which is left to the regulator.

Fixed Income

Interest on a security which is calculated as a constant specified percentage of the principal amount and paid at the end of specified interest periods, usually annually or semi-annually, until maturity.

Fixed-rate

A borrowing or investment where the interest or coupon paid is fixed throughout the arrangement.

Fixed Rate Borrowing

A fixed rate borrowing establishing the interest rate that will be paid throughout the life of the loan.

Flat Position

A position which has been fully closed out and no liability to make or take delivery exists.

Flat Yield (Also called the income yield)

The yield of a bond calculated as $\dfrac{\text{Annual Coupon}}{\text{Current market price}} \times 100\%$

Floating-rate

A borrowing or investment where the interest or coupon paid changes throughout the arrangement in line with some reference rate such as LIBOR.

Floating Rate Note (FRN)

Bond where each interest payment is made at the current or average market levels, often by reference to LIBOR.

Foreign Bond

Bond issued in a domestic market in the domestic currency and under the domestic rules of issuance by a foreign issuer (ex. Samurai bonds are bonds issued by issuers of other countries on the Japanese market).

Forex

Abbreviation for foreign exchange (currency trading).

Forward Rate Agreements (FRAs)

An agreement where the client can fix the rate of interest that will be applied to a notional loan or deposit, drawn or placed on an agreed date in the future, for a specified term.

Forward Delivery

Transactions which involve a delivery date in the future.

Forwards

Are very similar to futures contracts but they are not mainly traded on an exchange. They are not marked to market daily but settled only on the delivery date.

FSA

Financial Services Authority.

FT-SE 100 index

Main UK share index based on 100 leading shares.

Fund Manager

An organisation that invests money on behalf of someone else.

Fungibility

A futures contract with identical administration in more than one financial centre. Trades in various geographical locations can be off-set. (eg, bought on the IPE and sold on SGX).

Futures

An agreement to buy or sell an asset at a certain time in the future for a certain price.

Future Value

The amount of money which can be achieved at a given date in the future by investing (or borrowing) a given sum of money now at a given interest rate, assuming compound re-investment (or re-funding) of any interest payments received (or paid) before the end.

Gearing

The characteristic of derivatives which enables a far greater reward for the same, or much smaller, initial outlay. It is the ratio of exposure to investment outlay, and is also known as leverage.

General Principles

10 fundamental principles of behaviour written by FSA to apply all investment businesses.

Gilt

Domestic sterling-denominated long-term bond backed by the full faith and credit of the United Kingdom and issued by the Treasury.

Gilt Edged Market Makers (GEMMs)

A firm that is a market maker in gilts. Also known as a primary dealer.

Gilt Edged Security

UK government borrowing.

Give-Up

The process of giving a trade to a third party who will undertake the clearing and settlement of the trade.

Global Bond

A (temporary) certificate representing the whole of a bond issue.

Global Clearing

The channelling of the settlement of all futures and options trades through a single counterparty or through a number of counterparties geographically located.

Global Custodian

Institution that safekeeps, settles and performs processing of income collection, tax reclaim, multicurrency reporting, cash management, foreign exchange, corporate action and proxy monitoring etc. for clients' securities in all required marketplaces.

Global Depository Receipt (GDR)

A security representing shares held in custody in the country of issue.

GLOBEX

The overnight trading system operated by Reuters and the Chicago Mercantile Exchange (CME).

Good Delivery

Proper delivery of certificates that are negotiable and complete in terms of documentation or information.

Gross

A position which is held with both the bought and sold trades kept open.

Gross Domestic Product (GDP)

A measure of the country's entire output.

Gross Redemption Yield (GRY)

The annual return on owning a bond, allowing both for interest and profit on redemption.

Group of 30 (G30)

Private international organisation aiming to deepen understanding of international economic and financial issues.

GSCC

Government Securities Clearing Corporation – clearing organisation for US Treasury securities.

Guaranteed Bond

Bonds on which the principal or income or both are guaranteed by another corporation or parent company in case of default by the issuing corporation.

Haircut

The discount applied to the value of collateral used to cover margins.

Hard Commodities

Commodities such as tin or zinc. Futures on them are traded on the London Metal Exchange.

Hedge Ratio

Determining the ratio of the futures to the cash position so as to reduce price risk.

Hedging

A trading method which is designed to reduce or mitigate risk.

Reducing the risk of a cash position in the futures instrument to offset the price movement of the cash asset. A broader definition of hedging includes using futures as a temporary substitute for the cash position.

Holder

A person who has bought an open derivatives contract.

Home state regulation

Under the ISD, an investment business is authorised in the place of its head office and registered office. This home state authorisation entitles it to conduct business in any member state of the European Union.

Host State Regulation

Any European investment business operating outside its home basis is regulated by its host for its Conduct of business.

ICOM

International Currency Options Market standard documentation for netting foreign exchange option settlements.

Immobilisation

The storage of securities certificates in a vault in order to eliminate physical movement of certificates/documents in transfer of ownership.

Implied Repo Rate

The rate of return before financing costs implied by a transaction where a longer-term cash security is purchased and a futures contract is sold (or vice versa).

Independent Clearing Organisation

The independent organisation is quite separate from the actual members of the exchange, and will guarantee to each member the performance of the contracts by having them registered in the organisation's name.

Inflation

A period of generally rising prices.

Index Funds

Unit trusts which invest in the constituent parts of an index.

Index linked bond

Bond whose interest payment and redemption value are linked to the retail prices index.

Indirect Market Participation

Non-broker/dealers, such as institutional investors, who are active investors/traders.

Initial Margin

The deposit which the clearing house calls as protection against a default of a derivatives contract. It is returnable to the clearing member once the position is closed. The level is subject to changes in line with market conditions.

Insider Dealing

The criminal offence whereby those with unpublished price sensitive information deal, advise others to deal or pass the information on. Maximum penalty is seven years jail and an unlimited fine.

Institutional investor

An institution which is usually investing money on behalf of others. Examples are mutual funds and pension funds.

Integration

The third stage of money laundering, in which the money is finally integrated into the legitimate economy. See placement, layering.

Interbank Market

A market for transactions exclusively or predominantly within the banking system. In most countries, the market for short term money is an Interbank market since banks borrow and lend among one and another in order to balance their books on a daily basis. Non-bank entities may or may not be permitted to participate.

Inter Dealer Broker (IDB)

Member of the London Stock Exchange that acts as a link between firms to enable them to trade with each other anonymously.

Interest Rate Futures

Based on a debt instrument such as a Government Bond or a Treasury Bill as the underlying product and require the delivery of a bond or bill to fulfil the contract.

Interest Rate Swap

An agreement to exchange interest related payments in the same currency from fixed rate into floating rate (or vice versa) or from one type of floating rate to another.

Interim dividend

Dividend paid part way through a year in advance of the final dividend.

International Depository Receipt (IDR)

Receipt of shares of a foreign corporation held in the vaults of a depository bank. The receipt entitles the holder to all dividends and capital gains. Dividends and capital gains are converted to local currency as part of the service. IDRs allow investors to purchase foreign shares without having to involve themselves in foreign settlements and currency conversion.

International Equity

An equity of a company based outside the UK but traded internationally.

International Petroleum Exchange (IPE)

Market for derivatives of petrol and oil products.

International Standards Organisation (ISO)

An international federation of organisations of various industries which seeks to set common international standards in a variety of fields.

International Securities Identification (ISIN)

A coding system developed by the ISO for identifying securities. ISINs are designated to create one unique worldwide number for any security. It is a 12-digit alpha/numeric code.

Interpolation

The estimation of a price or rate, usually for a broken date, from two other rates or prices, each of which is for a date either side of the required date.

Intra-Day Margin

An extra margin call which the clearing organisation can call during the day when there is a very large movement up or down in the price of the contract.

Investment Services Directive (ISD)

European Union Directive imposing common standards on investment business.

Investment Business

Dealing, advising or managing investments. Those doing so need to be authorised.

Investments

Items defined in the FSA 86 to be regulated by it. Includes shares, bonds, options, futures, life assurance and pensions.

Investment Trust (Company)

A company whose sole function is to invest in the shares of other companies.

Invoice Amount

The amount calculated under the formula specified by the futures exchange which will be paid in settlement of the delivery of the underlying asset.

IOSCO

International Organisation of Securities Commissions.

IPMA

International Primary Markets Association.

Irredeemable Gilt

A gilt with no fixed date for redemption. Investors receive interest indefinitely.

ISDA

International Swaps and Derivatives Association, previously known as the International Swap Dealers Association. Many market participants use ISDA documentation.

ISMA

International Securities Markets Association.

ISSA

The International Securities Services Association.

Issue

Stocks or bonds sold by a corporation or government entity at a particular time.

Issue Price

The percentage of principal value at which the price of a new issue of securities is fixed.

Issuer

Legal entity that issues and distributed securities.

JASDEC

Japan Securities Depository Centre – the CSD for Japan.

JSCC

Japan Securities Clearing Corporation – clearing organisation in Japan.

Junk Bonds

High-risk bonds that have low ratings or are in default.

Last notice day

The final day that notification of delivery of a futures contract will be possible. On most exchanges all outstanding short futures contracts will be automatically delivered to open long positions.

Last trading day

Often the day preceding last notice day which is the final opportunity for holders of long derivatives positions to trade out of their positions and avoid ultimate delivery.

Layering

The second stage of money laundering, in which the money is passed through a series of transaction to obscure its origin. See placement, integration.

LCH

London Clearing House.

Lead Managers

In the eurobond markets the description given to the securities house appointed to handle a new issue.

Leverage

The magnification of gains and losses by only paying for part of the underlying value of the instrument or asset; the smaller the amount of funds invested, the greater the leverage. It is also known as gearing.

LIBID

The London inter-bank bid rate. The rate at which one bank will lend to another.

LIBOR

The London inter-bank offered rate. It is the rate used when one bank borrows from another bank. It is the benchmark used to price many capital market and derivative transactions.

LIFFE

London International Financial Futures and Options Exchange.

LIFFE Connect

LIFFE electronic dealing system.

Limit Order

Type of order input into SETS. If not completed immediately the balance is displayed on the screen and forms the Order Book.

Line order

An order in which a customer sets the maximum price he is willing to pay as a buyer or the minimum price he is willing to accept as a seller.

Linked Forex

When the currency contract is purchased to cover the local cost of a security trade.

Liquidity

A liquid asset is one that can be converted easily and rapidly into cash without a substantial loss of value. In the money market, a security is said to be liquid if the spread between bid and asked price is narrow and reasonable size can be done at those quotes.

Liquidity risk

The risk that a bank may not be able to close out a position because the market is illiquid.

Listed company

Company which has been admitted to listing on a stock exchange and whose shares can then be dealt on that exchange.

Listing

Status applied for by companies whose securities are then listed on the London Stock Exchange and available to be traded.

Listing Rules

Rule book for listed companies which governs their behaviour. Commonly known as the Yellow Book.

Liquidity

Ease with which an item can be traded on the market. Liquid markets are described as deep.

Lloyds of London

World's largest insurance market.

Loan Stock

See *bonds*.

London Inter Bank Offer Rate (LIBOR)

Rate at which banks lend to each other which is often used as the benchmark for floating rate loans (FRNs).

London International Financial Futures and Options Exchange (LIFFE)

Market for trading in bond, interest rate, FT-SE 100 index and FT-SE Mid 250 index, futures, plus equity options and soft commodity derivatives.

London Metal Exchange (LME)

Market for trading in derivatives of metals such as copper, tin, zinc etc.

London Stock Exchange (LSE)

Market for trading in securities. Formerly know as the International Stock Exchange of the United Kingdom and Republic of Ireland or ISE.

Long Coupons

1. Bonds or notes with a long current maturity;
2. A coupon on which the period is longer than the others or the standard coupon period.

Long-dated

Gilts with more than 15 years until redemption.

Long Position

Refers to an investor's account in which he has more shares of a specific security than he needs to meet his settlement obligations. Also a bought position in a derivative which is held open.

Lot

The common term used to describe the standard unit of trading for futures and options. It is also referred to as a "contract".

Mandatory event

A corporate action which affects the securities without giving any choice to the security holder.

Mandatory Quote Period

Time of day during which market makers in equities are obliged to quote prices under London Stock Exchange rules.

Margin

Initial margin is collateral placed by one party with a counterparty or clearing house at the time of a deal, against the possibility that the market price will move against the first party, thereby leaving the counterparty with a credit risk.

Variation margin is a payment made, or collateral transferred, from one party to the other because the market price of the transaction or of collateral has changed. Variation margin payment is either in effect a settlement of profit/loss (for example in the case of a futures contract) or the reduction of credit exposure.

In a loan, margin is the extra interest above a benchmark such as LIBOR required by a lender to compensate for the credit risk of that particular borrower.

Mark-To-Market

The process of revaluing an OTC or exchange traded product each day.

It is the difference between the closing price on the previous day against the current closing price. For exchange traded products this is referred to as variation margin.

Market

Description of any organisation or facility through which items are traded. All exchanges are markets.

Market Counterparty

A person dealing as agent or principal with the broker and involved in the same nature of investment business as the broker. This also includes fellow members of the SFA or trading members of an investment exchange, for those products only where they are members.

Market Forces

Supply and demand allowing buyers and sellers to fix the price without external interference.

Market Maker

A trader who works for an organisation such as an investment bank. They quote bids and offers in the market and are normally under an obligation to make a price in a certain number of contracts. They create liquidity in the contract by offering to buy or sell.

Market Price

In the case of a security, the market price is usually considered as the last reported price at which the stock or bond has been sold.

Market risk

Also position risk. The risk that the market value of a position falls.

Market Value

The price at which a security is trading and could presumably be purchased or sold.

Master Agreement

This agreement is for OTC transactions and is signed between the client and the broker. It covers the basic terms under which the client and broker wish to transact business. Each individual trade has a separate individual agreement with specific terms known as a confirm.

Matching (Comparison)

Another term for comparison (or checking); a matching system to compare trades and ensure that both sides of trade correspond.

Maturity

The date on which the principal or nominal value of a bond becomes due and payable in full to the holder.

Medium Dated

Gilts due to be redeemed within the next seven to fifteen years.

Mergers and Acquisition (M&A)

Divisions of securities houses or merchant banks responsible for advising on take-over activity. Usually work with the corporate finance department and is often kept as a single unit.

Mixed economy

Economy which relies on a mix of market forces and government involvement.

Model risk

The risk that the computer model used by a bank for valuation or risk assessment is incorrect or misinterpreted.

Model Code for Securities Dealing

Part of the Yellow Book that relates to directors dealing in their own company's securities. Prohibits them from doing so during the two months before results are announced.

Modified following

The convention that if a settlement date in the future falls on a non-business day, the settlement date will be moved to the next following business day, unless this moves it to the next month, in which case the settlement date is moved back to the last previous business day.

Money Market

The market for the purchase and sale of short-term financial instruments. Short term is usually defined as less than one year.

Money Market Fund

An open-end mutual fund which invests in commercial paper, banker's acceptances, repurchase agreements, government securities, and other highly liquid and safe securities. The fund pays money market rates of interest. Many money market funds are part of fund families; investors can switch their money from one fund to another and back again without charge.

MOF

The Ministry of Finance, (Japan).

Moody's Investment Service

Located in New York City with its parent, Dun & Bradstreet, Moody's is one of the two most popular bond rating agencies in the US. The other agency is Standard and Poor's.

Mortgage

A form of security on borrowing commonly associated with home borrowing.

Mortgage-Backed Security

Security backed by an investment company that raises money from shareholders and invests it in stocks, bonds or other instruments (unit trust, investment fund, SICAV – BEVEK).

Multilateral netting

Trade between several counterparties in the same security are netted such that each counterparty makes only one transfer of cash or securities to another party or to a central clearing system. Handles only transactions due for settlement on the same day.

Mutual collateralisation

The deposit of collateral by both counterparties to a transaction.

NASDAQ

National Association of Securities Dealers Automated Quotation system.

Netting

Trading partners offset their positions thereby reducing the number of positions for settlement. Netting can be either *bilateral, multilateral* or *continuous net settlement.*

Net Asset Value (NAV)

In mutual funds, the market value of the fund share. It is common practice for an investment trust to compute its assets daily, or even twice a say, by totalling the closing market value of all securities and assets (ie, cash) owned. All liabilities are deducted, and the balance is divided by the number of share outstanding. The resulting figure is the net asset value per share.

Net Present Value

Also NPV. The net total of several present values (arising from cashflows at different future dates) added together, some of which may be positive and some negative.

New Issues

Company raised additional capital by issuing new securities. New issue is the name given to the bonds or stocks offered to investors for the first time.

Nikkei Dow Index

Main share index in Japan.

Nil paid rights price

Ex-rights price less the subscription price.

Nominal Amount

Value stated on the face of a security (principal value, par value). Securities processing: number of securities to deliver/receive.

Nominal value of a bond

The value at which the capital, or principal, of a bond will be redeemed by the issuer. Also called par value.

Nominal value of a share

The minimum price at which a share can be issued. Also called par value.

Nominee

An organisation that acts as the named owner of securities on behalf of a different beneficial owner who remains anonymous to the company.

Non-callable

Cannot be redeemed by the issuer for a stated period of time from date of issue.

Non clearing member

A member of an exchange who does not undertake to settle their derivatives business. This type of member must appoint a clearing member to register all their trades at the clearing organisation.

Non competitive bid

In an auction, bidding for a specific amount of securities without mentioning a price. Usually, the price paid will be equal to the average of the accepted competitive bids.

Non-cumulative preference share

If the company fails to pay a preference dividend the entitlement to the dividend is simply lost. There is no accumulation.

Non-deliverable forward

A foreign exchange forward outright where, instead of each party delivering the full amount of currency at settlement, there is a single net cash payment to reflect the change in value between the forward rates transacted and the spot rate two working days before settlement.

Normal Market Size (NMS)

Minimum size in which market makers must quote on LSE.

Nostro

A bank's nostro account is its currency account held at another bank.

Nostro reconciliation

Checking the entries shown on the bank's nostro account statement with the bank's internal records (the accounting ledgers) to ensure that they correspond exactly.

Note

Bonds issued with a relatively short maturity are often called notes.

Notional

Contracts for differences require a notional principal amount on which settlement can be calculated.

Novation

The process where registered trades are cancelled with the clearing members and substituted by two new ones - one between the clearing house and the clearing member seller, the other between the clearing house and the clearing member buyer.

NSCC

National Securities Clearing Corporation – clearing organisation for US shares.

OASYS

Trade Confirmation system for US brokers operated by Thomson Financial Services.

OATs

Obligations Assimilables du Tresor – a 7-10-year French Treasury bond.

Obligation netting

An arrangement to transfer only the net amount (of cash or a security) due between two or more parties, rather than transfer all amounts between the parties on a gross basis.

Off-balance sheet

A transaction whose principal amount is not shown on the balance sheet because it is a contingent liability or settled as a contract for differences.

Offer for Sale

Historically, the most popular form of new issue in the UK for companies bringing their securities to the stockmarket for the first time. The company offers its shares to the general public.

Offer Price

The price at which a trader or market maker is willing to sell a contract.

Office of Fair Trading (OFT)

Government department which advises the Secretary of State for Trade and Industry on whether or not a proposed takeover should be referred to the MMC for full investigation.

Offshore

Relates to locations outside the controls of domestic monetary, exchange and legislative authorities. Offshore may not necessarily be outside the national boundaries of a country. In some countries, certain banks or other institutions may be granted offshore status and thus be exempt from all or specific controls or legislation.

Omnibus Account

Account containing the holdings of more than one client.

On-balance sheet

A transaction whose principal amount is shown on the balance sheet.

On-line

Processing which is executed via an interactive input onto a PC or stationary terminal connected to a processing centre.

Open Economy

A country where there are no restrictions on trading with other countries.

Open Ended

Type of investment such as Unit Trusts or OEICs which can expand without limit

Open Ended Investment Company (OEIC)

New corporate structure introduced in 1997. It is a form of collective investment vehicle.

Open Outcry

The style of trading whereby traders face each other in a designated area such as a pit and shout or call their respective bids and offers. Hand signals are also used to communicate. It is governed by exchange rules.

Opening Trade

A bought or sold trade which is held open to create a position.

Open Interest

The number of contracts both bought and sold which remain open for delivery on an exchange. Important indicator for liquidity.

Open Position

The number of contracts which have not been off-set at the clearing organisation by the close of business.

Operational risk

The risk of losses resulting from inadequate systems and control, human errors or management failings.

Option

An option is in the case of the **buyer**; the right, but not the obligation, to take (call) or make (put) for delivery of the underlying product and in the case of the **seller**; the obligation to make or take delivery of the underlying product.

Option Premium

The sum of money paid by the buyer, for acquiring the right of the option. It is the sum of money received by the seller for incurring the obligation, having sold the rights, of the option. It is the sum of the intrinsic value and the time value.

Optional Dividend

Dividend that can be paid either in cash or in stock. The shareholders entitled to the dividend make the choice.

Options On Futures

These have the same characteristics as an option, the difference being that the underlying product is either a long or short futures contract. Premium is not exchanged as the contracts are marked to market each day.

Order driven market

A stock market where brokers acting on behalf of clients match trades with each other either on the trading floor of the exchange or through a central computer system.

Oversubscribed

Circumstances where people have applied for more shares than are available in a new issue.

Out-Trade

A trade which has been incorrectly matched on the floor of an exchange.

Over-The-Counter (OTC)

A one-to-one agreement between two counterparties where the specifications of the product are completely flexible and non-standardised.

Overnight Money

Money placed on the money market for repayment for the next day.

Panel on Takeovers and Mergers (PTM)

A non-statutory body comprising City institution which regulates take-over activities.

Par Value

See *Nominal Value*.

Pair Off

Back-to-back trade between two parties where settlement occurs only by exchanging the cash difference between the two parties.

Pari Passu

Without partiality. Securities that rank pari passu, rank equally with each other.

Paying agent

A bank which handles payment of interest and dividends on behalf of the issuer of a security.

Payment Date

Date on which a dividend or an interest payment is scheduled to be paid.

Pension Fund

Fund set up by a corporation, labour union, governmental entity or other organisation to pay the pension benefits of retired workers. Pension funds invest billions of dollars annually in the securities markets and are therefore major market players.

Perpetual bond

A bond which has no redemption date.

Placement

The first stage of money laundering, in which the money is passed placed in the banking system. See layering, integration.

Placing

Procedure used for new issues where a securities house contracts its own clients to offer them stock. It is almost always used for new issues of eurobonds and for equities on the London Stock Exchange more so since January 1996 when restrictions on their use were removed.

Plain Vanilla or Vanilla Swap

A swap which has a very basic structure.

Portfolio

List of investments held by an individual or company, or list of loans made by a bank or financial institution.

Power of Attorney

The legal authority for one party to sign for and act on behalf of another party.

Preference Shares

Shares that have preferential rights to dividends, usually a fixed sum, before dividends are paid out to ordinary shareholders. They usually carry no voting rights. The rights of preference shareholders are established in a company's articles of association and may differ between companies in a variety of ways.

Premium

An option premium is the amount paid up-front by the purchaser of the option to the writer.

Present value

The amount of money which needs to be invested (or borrowed) now at a given interest rate in order to achieve exactly a given cashflow in the future, assuming compound re-investment (or re-funding) of any interest payments received (or paid) before the end. See future value.

Pre-settlement

Checks and procedures undertaken immediately after execution of a trade prior to settlement.

Price/earnings Ratio

The share price of a company divided by its earnings per share. A high p/e ratio implies that the company is well thought of for its future prospects.

Price (Conversion) Factor

The price at which a bond would trade, per 1 nominal, to yield the notional coupon of the futures contract on the delivery day (or the first day in the deliverable month if this applies).

Primary Dealer

See *Gilt Edged Market Maker*.

Primary Market

Market for the placement of new securities such as international, domestic and foreign bond issues. Any subsequent resale or purchase is handled on the secondary market.

Principal protected product

An investment whose maturity value is guaranteed to be at least the principal amount invested initially.

Principal Trading

When a member firm of the London Stock Exchange buys stock from or sells stock to a non-member.

Principal-To-Principal Market

A market where the clearing house only recognises the clearing member as one entity, and not the underlying clients of the clearing member.

Principal Value

That amount inscribed on the face of a security and exclusive of interest or premium. The amount is the one used in the computation of interest due on such a security.

Private Customer

An individual person who is not acting in the course of carrying on investment business.

Private placement

Issue of securities that is offered to a limited number of investors.

Privatisation

Process whereby the government puts state owned industries into the private sector, eg, water, electricity. Usually involves an offer for sale of its shares.

Project A

The after hours trading system used by the CBOT.

Proprietary Trader

A trader who deals for an organisation such as an investment bank taking advantage of short term price movements as well as taking long term views on whether the market will move up or down.

Prospectus

See *Listing Particulars*

Put Option

An option that gives the buyer the right, but not the obligation, to sell a specified quantity of the underlying asset at a fixed price, on or before a specified date. The seller of a put option has the obligation (because they have sold the right) to take delivery of the underlying asset if the option is exercised by the buyer.

Quoted

Colloquial term for a security that is traded on the Stock Exchange.

Quote Driven

Dealing system where some firms accept the responsibility to quote buying and selling prices.

Rating

Evaluation of securities investment and credit risk by rating services such as Moody's or Standard and Poor's.

RCH

Recognised Clearing House under the Financial Services Act.

Real Time Gross Settlement

Gross settlement system where trades are settled continuously through the processing day – abbreviate to RTGS.

Realised profit

Profit which has arisen from a real sale.

Reconciliation

The comparison of a person's records of cash and securities position with records held by another party and the investigation and resolution of any discrepancies between the two sets of records.

Record Date

The date on which a securities holder must hold the securities in order to receive an income or entitlement.

Redemption

The purchase and cancellation of outstanding securities through a cash payment to the holder.

Redemption Price

A price at which bonds may be redeemed, or called, at the issuer's option, prior to maturity (often with a slight premium).

Registered Title

Form of ownership of securities where the owner's name appears on a register maintained by the company.

Registrar of Companies

Government department responsible for keeping records of all companies.

Replacement cost

The mark-to-market loss which would be incurred if it were necessary to undertake a new transaction to replace an existing one, because the existing counterparty defaulted.

Repurchase Agreement (Repo)

Borrowing funds by providing a government security for collateral and promising to 'repurchase' the security at the end of the agreed upon time period. The associated interest rate is the 'repo-rate'.

Reputational risk

The risk that an organisation's reputation will be damaged.

Reverse Repo

Purchase of gilt where the price and date for its re-sale is fixed at the same time.

RIE

Recognised Investment Exchange under the Financial Services Act.

Rights Issue

Offer of shares made to existing shareholders.

Right Of Offset

Where positions and cash held by the Clearing Organisation in different accounts for a member are allowed to be netted.

Risk Warning

Document that must be despatched and signed by private customers before they deal in traded options.

Roll-Over

A Libor fixing on a new tranche of loan, or transfer of a futures position to the next delivery month.

Rolling Settlement

System used in most countries including UK. Bargains are settled a set number of days after being transacted.

Round Lot

The minimum amount for which dealer's quotes are good.

Safekeeping

Holding of securities on behalf of clients. They are free to sell at any time.

Sale of rights nil paid

The sale of the entitlement to take up a rights issue – see also nil paid price.

Same Day Funds

Refers to the availability of funds on the same day as they are deposited.

Scrip Dividends

Scrip dividends options provide shareholders with the choice of receiving dividend entitlements in the form of cash, share or a combination or both. The amount of stocks to be distributed under a scrip option is calculated by dividing the cash dividend amount by the average market price over a recent period of time.

SEATS Plus

An order-driven system used on the London Stock Exchange for securities which do not attract at least two firms of market makers and for all AIM securities.

Secondary Market

Market place for trading in existing securities. The price at which they are trading has no direct effect on the company's fortunes but is a reflection of investors' perceptions of the company.

Securities

Bonds and equities.

Securities House

General term covering any type of organisation involved in securities although usually reserved for the larger firms.

Securities Lending

Loan of securities by an investor to another (usually a broker-dealer), usually to cover a short sale.

SEDOL

Stock Exchange Daily Official List, a securities numbering system assigned by the International Stock Exchange in London.

Segregated account

Account in which there is only the holdings of one client.

Segregation Of Funds

Where the client assets are held separately from those assets belonging to the member firm.

SEQUAL

The checking system used for international equities.

SETS

Stock Exchange Electronic Trading Service. The electronic order book used by the London Stock Exchange.

Settlement

The fulfilment of the contractual commitments of transacted business.

Settlement Date

The date on which a trade is cleared by delivery of securities against funds (actual settlement date, contractual settlement date).

17F-5

Legal requirements for world-wide correspondent banks which serve US mutual funds, pension funds and other regulated financial groups.

Share Futures

Based on individual shares. Delivery is fulfilled by the payment or receipt of cash against the exchange calculated delivery settlement price.

Share Option

A right sold to an investor conferring the option to buy or sell shares of a particular company at a predetermined price and within a specified time limit.

Short

A sold position in a derivative which is held open.

Short Coupons

Bonds or notes with a short current maturity.

Short Cover

The purchase of a security that has been previously sold short. The purpose is to return securities that were borrowed to make a delivery.

Short-dated Gilt

Gilts due to be redeemed within the next seven years, according to the LSE, (FT states up to 5 years).

Short Sale

The sale of securities not owned by the seller in the expectation that the price of these securities will fall or as part of an arbitrage.

Short Selling

Selling stock that you do not own.

Short-term Security

Generally an obligation maturing in less than one year.

Soft Commodities

Description given to commodities such as sugar, coffee and cocoa, traded through LIFFE since its incorporation of the former London Commodity Exchange (LCE).

Sovereign Debt Securities

Bonds issued by the government of a country.

SPAN

Standardised Portfolio Analysis of Risk. A form of margin calculation for derivatives which is used by various clearing organisations.

Speculator

The speculator is a trader who wants to assume risk for potentially much higher rewards.

Sponsored Member

Type of CREST member whose name appears on the register but has no computer link with CREST.

Spot delivery

A delivery or settlement of currencies on the value date, two business days later.

Spot Market

Market for immediate as opposed to future delivery. In the spot market for foreign exchange, settlement is in two business days ahead.

Spread

The difference between the bid and offer rate. Also describes a trade in more than one delivery month or more than one product.

A trading strategy in which a trader buys one instrument and sells another, related instrument with a view to profiting from a change in the price difference between the two. A futures spread is the purchase of one futures contract and the sale of another; an option spread is the purchase of one call (or put) and the sale of another.

Stamp duty

Tax on purchase of equities in the UK.

Stamp Duty Reserve Tax (SDRT) (UK)

Tax payable on the purchase of UK equities in uncertified form (ie, those held within CREST).

Standard Settlement Instructions

Instructions for settlement with a particular counterparty which are always followed for a particular kind of deal and, once in place, are therefore not repeated at the time of each transaction.

Standing Instruction

Default instruction, eg, provided to an agent processing payments or clearing securities trades; provided by shareholder on how to vote shares (for example, vote for all management recommended candidates).

Stepped

A stepped coupon is one which rises or falls in a pre-determined way over the life of an arrangement.

Stock

In some countries (eg, US.), the term applies to ordinary share capital of a company. In other countries (eg, UK), stock ma mean share capital that is issued in variable amount instead of in fixed specified amounts, or it can describe government loans.

Stock Dividend

Dividends paid by a company in stock instead of cash.

Stock Exchange Automated Quotation System (SEAQ)

Electronic screen display system through which market makers in equities display prices at which they are willing to deal.

Stock Exchange Electronic Trading System (SETS)

Description usually given to the London Stock Exchange.

Stock Index Futures / Options

Based on the value of an underlying stock index like the FTSE 100 in the UK, the S & P 500 index in the US and the Nikkei 225 and 300 in Japan. Delivery is fulfilled by the payment or receipt of cash against the exchange calculated delivery settlement price.

These are referred to as both indices or indexes.

Stock (or Bond) Power

A legal document, either on the back of registered stocks and bonds or attached to them, by which the owner assigns his interest in the corporation to a third party, allowing that party the right to substitute another name on the company records instead of the originals owner's.

Stock Split

When a corporation splits its stock, it divides.

Street Name

Securities held in street name are held in the name of a broker or another nominee ie, a customer.

Strike price

The fixed price, per share or unit, at which an option conveys the right to call (purchase) or put (sell) the underlying shares or units.

Stripped Bonds (Strips)

Bonds where the rights to the interest payments and eventual repayment of the nominal value have been separated from each other and trade independently. Facility introduced for gilts in December 1997.

Subcustodian

A bank in a foreign country that acts on behalf of the custodian as its custody agent.

Subscription Price

Price at which shareholders of a corporation are entitled to purchase common shares in a rights offering or at which subscription warrants are exercisable.

Straight-through processing

Computer transmission of the details of a trade, without manual intervention, from their original input by the trader to all other relevant areas – position keeping, risk control, accounts, settlement, reconciliation.

Strike price/rate

Also exercise price. The price or rate at which the holder of an option can insist on the underlying transaction being fulfilled.

Strip

The purchase or sale of a series of consecutive interest rate futures contracts or forward rate agreements.

Swap

Arrangement where two borrowers, one of whom has fixed interest and one of whom has floating rate borrowings, swap their commitments with each other. A bank would arrange the swap and charge a fee.

SwapClear

A clearing house and central counterparty for swaps.

SwapsWire

An electronic dealing system for swaps.

SWIFT

Society for Worldwide Interbank Financial Telecommunications – secure electronic communications network between banks.

Syndicate

A group of bond houses which act together in underwriting and distributing a new securities issue.

TARGET

Trans European Automated Real time Gross settlement Express Transfer – system linking the real-time gross settlements for euros in the 15 European Union countries.

TechMark

Market on the LSE for technology related stocks.

Tender Offer

Formal offer to buy made to holders of a particular issue by a third party. Detailed offer is made by public announcement in newspapers and sometimes by personal letter of transmittal to each stockholder.

Thomson Report

An electronic transaction reporting system for international equities on the London Stock Exchange operated by Thomson.

Tick Size

The value of a one point movement in the contract price of a derivative.

Touch

The best prices available for a stock on the stockmarket, looking at all market makers.

Trade Guarantees

Guarantees in place in a market which ensure that all compared or netted trades will be settled as compared regardless of a counterparty default.

Traded Option

An option which is traded on an exchange.

Trader

An individual who buys and sells securities with the objective of making short-term gains.

Trading Permits

These are issued by exchanges and give the holder the right to have one trader at any one time trading in the contract(s) to which the permit relates.

Transfer Agent

Agent appointed by a corporation to maintain records of stock and bond owners, to cancel and issue certificates and to resolve problems arising from lost, destroyed or stolen certificates.

Transparency

The degree to which a market is characterised by prompt availability of accurate price and volume information which gives participants comfort that the market is fair.

TRAX

Trade confirmation system for the Euro-markets operated by ISMA.

Treasury Bill

Money market instrument issued with a life of less than one year issued by the US and UK governments.

Treasury Bonds (US)

US government bond issued with a 30 year maturity.

Treasury Notes (US)

US government bond issued with 2-, 3-, 5- and 7- year maturity.

Trustee

Are appointed to oversee the management of certain funds. They are responsible for ensuring that the fund is managed correctly and that the interest of the investor are protected and that all relevant regulations and legislation are complied with.

Turnaround

Securities bought and sold for settlement on the same day.

Two-way Price

Simultaneous prices in a stock quoted by a market maker, the lower at which he is willing to buy and the higher at which he is willing to sell.

Underlying Asset

The asset from which the future or option's price is derived.

Underwriters

Institutions which agree to take up shares in a new issue if it is undersubscribed. They will charge an underwriting fee.

Unit Trust

A system whereby money from a number of investors is pooled together and invested collectively on their behalf. Each owns a unit (or number of them) the value of which depends on the value of those items owned by the trust.

Unrealised profit

Profit which has not arisen from a sale – an increase in value of an asset.

Value at Risk (VaR)

The maximum amount which a bank expects to lose, with a given confidence level, over a given time period.

Variation Margin

The process of revaluing an exchange traded derivative product each day.

It is the difference between the closing price on the previous day against the current closing price. It is physically paid or received each day by the clearing organisation. It is often referred to as the mark-to-market.

Volatility

The degree of scatter of the underlying price when compared to the mean average rate.

Vostro

A vostro account is another bank's account held at ourbank in our currency.

Warrants

An option which can be listed on an exchange, with a lifetime of generally more than one year.

Warrant agent

A bank appointed by the issuer as an intermediary between the issuing company and the (physical) warrant holders, interacting when the latter want to exercise the warrants.

Withholding Tax

In the securities industry, a tax imposed by a government's tax authorities on dividends and interest paid.

Writer

A person who has sold an open derivatives contract and is obliged to deliver or take delivery upon notification of exercise from the buyer.

XETRA

Dealing system of the Deutsche Börse.

Yankee bond

A US dollar bond issued in the USA by a non-USA corporation.

Yield

Internal rate of return expressed as a percentage.

Yield Curve

For securities that expose the investor to the same credit risk, a graph showing the relationship at a given point in the time between yield and current maturity. Yield curves are typically drawn using yields on governments bonds of various maturities.

Yield to Maturity

The rate of return yielded by a debt security held to maturity when both interest payments and the investor's capital gain or loss on the security are taken into account.

Zero coupon Bond

A bond issued with no coupon but a price substantially below par so that only capital is accrued over the life of the loan, and yield is comparable to coupon bearing instruments.

Appendices

Australian Financial Markets Association	www.afma.com
Australian Stock Exchange	www.asx.com.au
Bank for International Settlement	www.bis.org
Computer Based Learning Ltd	www.cbl-ltd.co.uk
Chicago Board Options Exchange	www.cboe.com
Chicago Board of Trade	www.cbot.com
Commodities Future Trading Commission	www.cftc.gov
Clearnet	www.clearnetsa.com
Clearstream	www.clearstream.com
Chicago Mercantile Exchange	www.cme.com
CRESTCo	www.crestco.co.uk
Depository Trust Company	www.dtc.org
European Central Securities Depositories Association	www.ecsda.com
EUREX	www.eurexchange.com
Euroclear	www.euroclear.com

Futures and Options Association	www.foa.co.uk
Futures Industry Association	www.fiafii.org
Financial Services Agency Japan	www.fsa.go.jp
Financial Services Authority	www.fsa.gov.uk
Hong Kong Exchanges and Clearing	www.hkex.com.hk
International Securities Markets Association	www.isma.co.uk
International Securities Services Association	www.issanet.org
London Clearing House	www.lch.co.uk
London International Financial Futures & Options Exchange	www.liffe.com
London Metal Exchange	www.lme.co.uk
London Stock Exchange	www.londonstockexchange.com
Nasdaq	www.nasdaq.com
Norex Alliance	www.norex.com
New York Stock Exchange	www.nyse.com
G30 Recommendations	http://risk.ifci.ch/
Securities Exchange Commission (US)	www.sec.gov
Securities Institute	www.securities-institute.org.uk
Singapore Exchange	www.ses.com.sg
Tokyo Stock Exchange	www.tse.or.jp
virt-x	www.virtx.com

SECURITIES INSTITUTE PUBLISHING

Each publication provides a detailed overview and practical introduction to key topics within financial services.

The two titles in our *Essential Elements* series – EMU and Money Laundering – provide rapid briefing on key issues as they arise. Each booklet contains the relevant facts and figures to give you an overview of the subject.

Our *Griffin Guide* range consists of re–worked and updated notes from our popular courses. These publications are a useful reference for everyone who needs to grasp the basics of a topic – fast!

To place an order or find out more, call now on *020 7645 0680*.

Essential Elements

ESSENTIAL ELEMENTS OF THE PREVENTION OF MONEY LAUNDERING

This quick guide looks at the scale of the problem and efforts taken to overcome it: an essential reference for all who are concerned to identify attempts at money laundering within their organisation.

- What is money laundering?
- Money laundering and the law
- How do you spot it in the process, and what to do.

48PP PAPERBACK, ISBN: 1 84307 005 7, 2ND EDITION

THE ESSENTIAL ELEMENTS OF ECONOMIC & MONETARY UNION

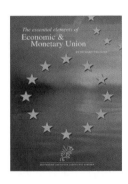

Economic and Monetary Union (EMU) is the system that links together the economies and currencies of the participating European countries. The European Central Bank has become responsible for centralised monetary policy. What does the Euro mean for you?

- Convergence
- Impact of the Euro on the markets
- Preparing for the future.

28PP PAPERBACK, ISBN: 1 900520 31 1

Griffin Guides

UNDERSTANDING REGULATION & COMPLIANCE

Understanding Regulation & Compliance outlines the
new regulatory structure in the post-N2 environment.
It describes the new powers of FSA and the
requirements placed upon individuals and firms to
ensure their compliance. Topics include:

- The Financial Services & Markets Act 2000
- The Financial Services Authority
- The FSA Handbook
- Conduct of business rules
- Client assets
- Improper dealings
- Money laundering

240PP PAPERBACK, ISBN: 1 843070 07 3

AN INTRODUCTION TO CORPORATE FINANCE
- TRANSACTIONS AND TECHNIQUES

Introduction to Corporate Finance provides readers
with the key elements of corporate finance. The book
introduces the principle techniques used in corporate
finance, combined with practical experience and
hands-on, numerically orientated case studies.

- Sources of Capital
- Flotations/Initial Public Offerings
- Mergers and Acquisitions
- Management Buy Outs
- Determining the Cost of Capital
- International Equity Offerings
- Valuing Securities
- Well illustrated with diagrams and tables, bullet points and summaries.

96PP PAPERBACK, ISBN: 1 900520 09 5

AN INTRODUCTION TO SWAPS

An Introduction to Swaps gives a detailed overview of how the various categories of swap work, how they are traded and what they are used for. Topics include interest rate swaps, managing risk, asset swaps, currency swaps. The book is illustrated with over 50 diagrams and tables.

- Managing risk with swaps
- Asset swaps
- Currency swaps.

160PP PAPERBACK, ISBN: 1 900520 21 4

AN INTRODUCTION TO FUND MANAGEMENT

An Introduction to Fund Management introduces readers to the economic rationale for the existence of funds, the different types available, investment strategies and many other related issues from the perspective of the investment manager. Topics include the features and characteristics of funds, portfolio management and administration, performance measurement and investment mathematics. Includes relevant formulae, equations and examples.

- Features and characteristics of funds
- Portfolio management and administration
- Performance measurement
- Investment mathematics.

160PP PAPERBACK, ISBN: 1 84307 022 7, 2ND EDITION

AN INTRODUCTION TO VALUE–AT–RISK

An Introduction to Value–at–Risk has been written for those with little or no previous understanding of or exposure to the concepts of risk management and Value–at–Risk. Topics include applications of VaR, instrument structures, stress testing, VaR for corporates, credit risk and legal/regulatory issues.

- Risk and Risk management
- VaR and Derivatives, Fixed Interest products.
- VaR for Corporates

208PP PAPERBACK, ISBN: 1 900520 63 X, 2ND EDITION

INTRODUCTION TO EQUITY MARKETS

Introduction to Equity Markets provides an overview of the current financial services industry. The book introduces the reader to different types of companies and shares as well as analysis of UK markets. An overview of dealing and settlement in some of the world's major markets is also featured. Contents include:

- Shareholders and Company Law
- Issuing Shares – The Primary Market
- Trading Shares – The Secondary Market
- Settlement of Transactions
- Major Overseas Exchanges and Indices
- Dividends, Bonus Issues and Rights Issues
- Company Accounts.

170PP PAPERBACK, ISBN: 1 900520 71 0

INTRODUCTION TO REPO MARKETS

An Introduction to Repo Markets provides a
comprehensive description and analysis of the repo
markets. The text has been written to cater for those with
little or no previous experience of the repo markets, though
it also develops the subject matter to sufficient depth to be
of use to more experienced practitioners. Contents include:

- Uses and economic functions of repo
- Accounting, Tax and Capital issues
- The UK gilt repo market
- The implied repo rate and basis trading
- Repo and the yield curve

240PP PAPERBACK, ISBN: 1 900520 86 9 2ND EDITION

INTRODUCTION TO BOND MARKETS

Introduction to Bond Markets provides a comprehensive,
authoritative description and analysis of the bond markets.
The book considers basic 'plain vanilla' bonds and
elementary bond mathematics, before looking at the array
of different instruments available. Contents include:

- Bond Yield Measurement
- Corporate Debt Markets
- Eurobonds
- Introduction to Repo
- Risk Management
- Off–Balance Sheet Instruments
- Government Bond Markets
- Emerging Bond Markets.

410PP PAPERBACK, ISBN: 1 900520 79 6, 2ND EDITION

INTRODUCTION TO THE GILT STRIPS MARKET

Introduction to the Gilt Strips Market provides a thorough description and analysis of gilt strips. The contents describe and define strips as a financial instrument and examine the use and application of gilt strips within the context of the capital markets as a whole. Contents include:

- Zero–coupon bonds
- The yield curve
- Interest rate risk for strips
- Settlement, tax and regulatory issues
- Trading and strategy

192PP PAPERBACK, ISBN: 1 84307 006 5, 2ND EDITION

DICTIONARY OF FINANCIAL & SECURITIES TERMS

This updated and greatly expanded 2nd edition gives definitions of frequently used terms in the financial and securities industry including new N2 terminology. Also included is a comprehensive listing of abbreviations, acronyms and industry websites.

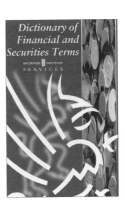

- What is a Bill of Exchange?
- What does SPAN stand for?
- What are CHIPS and CHAPS?
- What is the standard definition of EPS?

Over 2,500 entries. Included with the dictionary is a FREE CD–ROM version for users to load onto their PC for easy reference at home or at work.

APPROX 400PP PAPERBACK, ISBN: 1 84307 023 5, 2ND EDITION

THE FUNDAMENTALS OF CREST

The Fundamentals of CREST gives a detailed overview of securities administration and settlement through the CREST system. It is illustrated throughout with diagrams and tables, bullet points and summaries.

- Handling Certificated Securities
- Corporate Actions and Claims
- Stock Loans and Collateral.

128PP PAPERBACK, ISBN: 1 900520 98 2 2ND EDITION

For further details on these and other new titles, contact our Client Services Department on 020 7645 0680

Forthcoming titles

RETAIL PUBLICATIONS

- Advanced Operations Management
- Futures, Options and Other Derivatives Products
- Products, Trading and Operations
- Custody, Stock Lending and Derivatives Clearing
- Risk Management
- Clearing Settlement and Custody Operations
- Products and Trading from an Operations Perspective
- Mutual Funds

SECURITIES INSTITUTE GLOBAL CAPITAL MARKETS SERIES

- IPO and Equity Offerings
- Controls, Procedures and Risk
- Clearing, Settlement and Custody
- Managing Technology in the Operations Function
- Relationship and Resource Management in Operations
- Understanding the Markets
- Credit Risk

For further information on this series please call 01865 888180 or visit http://www.bh.com/finance/

We plan to introduce new titles into our retail range in the forthcoming year. All the titles listed are provisional and may be subject to alteration.

n on or before